THE GOD LIFE
LIVING BEYOND THE ORDINARY

A 90-DAY DEVOTIONAL BY

JANET BRAZEE

FOREWORD BY MARK BRAZEE

The body of Christ has been blessed with many teachers and preachers in the pulpit, and we're used to those ministry gifts. The teacher is instructional and the preacher is inspirational, and the Church needs both. But there's another ministry gift described in Romans 12 that the body of Christ has not experienced nearly enough—the exhorter. Exhortation works by inspiration. On the spur of the moment, the Holy Ghost will inspire the exhorter to encourage and sometimes even to correct. It's a valuable gift.

For years I've watched God use Janet in this gift time and time again, and it's been a great blessing. We've always ministered as a team, and even in the early days of our ministry, Janet would sing a song or two and exhort a little before turning over services to me. But especially as we've pastored World Outreach Church, where Janet leads praise and worship, she's really stepped in to the fullness of this gift because there's a platform and a place for it.

Janet doesn't sit home studying and preparing mini messages for each service, and yet, just about every service I watch the Holy Ghost come on her to exhort with a message from heaven. I've heard Janet say that God uses her as a spoon, and for sure, by the Holy Ghost she stirs up believers with words from heaven and encourages them.

I don't remember one time in 35 years of ministry when Janet has exhorted that people have not told us afterward the message was exactly what they needed to hear. I pray that the exhortations throughout this book will be exactly what *you* need to hear and will stir you up and encourage you to live *The God Life*.

THE GOD LIFE—Living Beyond the Ordinary

978-0-9891429-6-0

Published by Mountz Media & Publishing

Tulsa, Oklahoma

918-296-0995

www.mountzmedia.com

CONTENTS

INTRODUCTION

God never intended for you and I to lead dull, ordinary, defeated lives on this earth. In fact, God sent Jesus Christ to give every one of us abundant life here and now and eternity with Him ever after. God's idea of abundance for you and I is *zoe*, which in the Greek means *the God-kind of life*. God's design is that we lead lives so supernatural, so blessed, so amazing that the only way to describe it is *living beyond the ordinary*.

The word *ordinary*, according to The American Heritage Dictionary, means *commonly encountered, usual, the normal condition*. So, in other words, ordinary is the exact opposite of the life God has in mind for you.

God wants your life to be extraordinary, which according to the dictionary means *extraordinary, beyond the ordinary or usual, highly exceptional, remarkable, employed or used for a special service, function, or occasion*. That's more like it. *The God Life* is anything but normal.

Consider Jesus. His entire life was highly exceptional, remarkable and definitely used for a special service. Jesus lived His life out of the box and full of the supernatural, and He intends for us to do the same.

The truth is, if your life seems boring and ordinary, you simply have not tapped into *The God Life* you were meant to live. Nothing about your life should be mundane. This earth and everything in it was made for you. You were told to rule and reign. God has given you purpose and power to carry it out, so living beyond the ordinary is not pie in the sky. It's an achievable lifestyle. You can do it. It's your destiny.

God's plan is that we live beyond the ordinary every day of the week from morning until night. After all, God lives in us, and 1 Corinthians 3:16 says we are temples of the living God. If we are born-again and Spirit-filled, we are wall-to-wall God on the inside. Greater is He that's in us than he that's in the world (1 John 4:4). Christ in us, the hope of Glory (Colossians 1:27).

There's no question about it, we're filled with the life of God. So it's time we act like it.

It's time the God inside of us shows up on the outside of us.

It's time you and I set aside sin, religious traditions, ruts, opinions, laziness, selfishness or anything else that holds us back and hinders us and go a whole new way. So whether you're 18 or 80, don't waste your life living below God's best for you. Walk a new way! Come up higher! If you're already walking a deep and mature walk with Jesus, there's still a deeper and more mature walk available because there's always more of Him available.

I pray that as you read the pages of this book, you'll take them to heart. Read them more than once. Let the words soak in and bring change from the inside out. If there's a scripture text, meditate on it. When there's an action step recommended, do it. Then apply the revelation He brings you so that you may come to know the Greater One even greater still. I pray that you will go from glory to glory to yet another glory. I pray that you live *The God Life*.

~ Janet

① | COME RIGHT ON IN!

Every single thing you'll ever need is waiting on you in the presence of God. Psalm 16:11 tells us that in God's presence there is fullness of joy and at His right hand are pleasures forevermore. The only thing that's left for us to do is tap into His presence and take hold of the blessings He has for us.

Best yet, we can go boldly into His presence anytime, day or night, 24/7. We don't have to wait for a high priest to go in for us like the Israelites in the Old Testament. We don't have to wait for our pastor to go first and pave the way for us. We don't have to wait for our prayer group or small group or any other group. You and I are welcome in the throne room where God is always saying to us, "Come right on in! I've been waiting for you!" His arms are always wide open.

He never says, "I don't have time for you right now." He never says, "Come back later." He never says, "My secretary will take care of you." He never says, "Your problems are too complicated and too messy for me." No. He says, "Come to Me, all you who labor and are heavy laden, and I will give you rest" (Matthew 11:28). The Message says, "Are you tired? Worn out? Burned out on religion? Come to me. Get away with me and you'll recover your life. I'll show you how to take a real rest. Walk with me and work with me—watch how I do it....I won't lay anything heavy or ill-fitting on you. *Keep company with me and you'll learn to live freely and lightly*" (28-30).

We're always welcome to come into His presence, and when we come out, we'll never be the same again.

ACTION ▷ ···

Read Hebrews 4:16 in a few different translations. Declare aloud to your Father what a privilege it is to be welcomed into His throne room. Then go on in for a visit!

(2) | LIVING BEYOND THE ORDINARY

I came so they can have real and eternal life,
more and better life than they ever dreamed of.
John 10:10 The Message

God has big plans for you. His plan is better than anything you've ever dreamed for yourself. In fact, God's whole purpose in sending Jesus to the earth was to give you abundant life. He wants to teach you and lead you to be healthy, wealthy and wise. But hold on. The devil has big plans for you, too. Jesus came to give you abundant life, but the devil comes to steal, to kill and to destroy (John 10:10).

The difference between God's plans and the devil's is huge, and it's not hard to figure out what's what. It's an easy line to draw in the sand. In fact, each of us should draw the line so we don't go through life unable to trust God in the face of trouble, wondering, "Is this situation, circumstance or symptom that has come against me caused by God or the devil?"

Let me make it simple. God is life. If something is good, true, perfect and right, it's from God. If something steals, kills and destroys, it's from the devil. Don't let anybody tell you different because God never teaches you through sickness, lack or trouble. Frankly, it's not His style. The Bible tells us that the Holy Ghost is the teacher of the Church, and He teaches us with the Word of God.

So how do we get God's Word off the page and producing abundant life for us? Second Peter 1:4 says God has given us "…exceedingly great and precious promises, that through these you may be partakers of the divine nature." We take hold of God's promises by taking hold of His Word. We need to find out what God's Word says about our lives, our circumstances and our futures, and then we need to open our mouths in faith and agree with God. Then the Bible says we can be of good cheer, for it will be even as God said it would be (Acts 27:25).

ACTION ▷ ....

Are you facing situations, circumstances or symptoms that aren't life beyond the ordinary? If so, write the situation in the left column, and write how God says it should be in the right column. Begin to say what God says.

SITUATIONS AND CIRCUMSTANCES	WHAT GOD SAYS

③ | SUPERMAN AND WONDER WOMAN

For you are still [unspiritual, having the nature] of the flesh [under the control of ordinary impulses]. For as long as [there are] envying and jealousy and wrangling and factions among you, are you not unspiritual and of the flesh, behaving yourselves after a human standard and like mere (unchanged) men?
1 Corinthians 3:3 AMP

We just read what the apostle Paul had to say about how Christians should behave, and believe it or not, one thing he said is that we should not act like humans. Paul said we should not behave ourselves "*after a human standard … like mere (unchanged) men.*" The word *mere* means *being nothing more than what is expected.* In other words, Paul was explaining that God does not want us to be mere men and women. God does not want us to live ordinary lives.

The truth is, mere people don't expect much out of life, and what they do expect isn't all that grand. Most mere people expect to get the flu this year. Many say, "I get the flu every year, so why would this year be any different?" Most mere people expect to run out of money before their monthly bills are paid. Mere men and women expect the worst; they expect their lives to function according to the world's unusually low standards. Yet, Jesus came to pluck us out of the mere-men-and-women mentality and set our feet on much higher ground.

So why would anybody live on low ground? Paul explains why in 1 Corinthians 3, drawing an important connection between carnality and the lives of mere men and women. Most Christians connect carnality with blatant, outright sin, and that's true enough. But it's not the whole story. The word *carnal* comes from the same Greek word as *carnivorous,* which means *meat or flesh eating.* Therefore, a carnal Christian is ruled by his or her flesh or body cravings.

For example, a carnal Christian attends church on Sunday morning if he or she *feels* like it. If the person doesn't feel like it, he or she rolls over and snores away. Is that a sin? Well, I wouldn't call it sin, but I would call it being carnal because the decision was dominated by what the body wants.

Many scriptures talk about carnality and most of us are pretty familiar with the list. Truly, we all have carnal moments—that's life on Earth. But Romans 8:5-8 says, "For they that are after the flesh do mind the things of the flesh; but they that are after the Spirit the things of the Spirit. For to be carnally minded is death; but to be spiritually minded is life and peace. Because the carnal mind is enmity against God: for it is not subject to the law of God, neither indeed can be. So then they that are in the flesh cannot please God" (KJV).

God has a better—more abundant—not-at-all-ordinary or carnal life for you. You are not a mere man. You are Superman. You are not a mere woman. You are Wonder Woman. You are born again, full of the Word and full of the Spirit. Jesus says as He is *so are you* in this world (1 John 4:17).

ACTION ▷ ···

Confession time between you and you. List below some of the ways you have given way to the flesh in the past. Once you see the list in black and white, it will make it hard to continue that way. And that's a good thing!

THE CARNAL WAY	THE GOD WAY

(4) | WWJD

When Jesus promised His followers abundant life, He promised them *zoe* or the God-kind of life. Jesus was talking about the very life, nature and ability of God Almighty that resides inside every Christian. He was talking about life so amazing the best word we can use to describe it is *divine*.

Actually, the word *divine* paints an excellent picture of the life God intended for us. It means *heavenly, God-like or preceding from God*. The life Jesus came to provide us is God-like because God imparted Himself to us; we're created in His image. You might have heard the old saying, "She's the spittin' image of her momma." Think about it. When people see us walking down the street, they should say, "Whoa—he or she is the spittin' image of God."

You are a living epistle known and read by all, whether you're having a good day or a bad day. How does your life read early Monday morning? How does it read by Friday afternoon? If you're letting God call the shots in your life, people should be reading divine life all over you all the time.

Yet, as we all know, each of us is confronted with choices all day long every day that determine whether or not we walk in divine life. In fact, the popular phrase WWJD—What Would Jesus Do?—could come in handy as you choose between right and wrong throughout your day. For example, do you overlook snippiness or become offended? Do you forget wrongs done to you? Do you get mad when you're cut off in traffic? Do you bite your tongue instead of having the last word?

Let me share with you the same good advice my momma gave me: "You can just get glad in the same pants you got mad in." She told me that countless times since I was a little girl, so I know how to get glad in the same pants I get mad in. You need to know, too. I get mad; we all do. But I've also learned how to get glad really quick. Don't think it's not a choice because *it is* a choice. How will you act as life confronts you? Let divine life rise up and answer for you.

ACTION ≫ ....

Admit to yourself a few times in the past week when you should have "gotten glad in the same pants you got mad in." Don't beat yourself up over it. Just figure out WWJD and choose His way next time.

_____

_____

_____

_____

_____

_____

_____

⑤ | GET OVER YOURSELF

We talked earlier about God wanting us to live a life so beyond the ordinary, so supernatural, so blessed and so amazing that the best word we can use to describe it is *divine*. So let's look at yet another definition of the word *divine*, which means *above human or moving past the natural into the supernatural*.

"Can I live in the supernatural?" someone might ask. Absolutely! You can because Philippians 4:13 says you can do ALL things through Jesus Christ who strengthens you. In and of yourself, you are full of limitations and you're able to think of hundreds of things you cannot imagine yourself doing even for God.

Somebody might say, *Me get on the platform to preach? No way! Me with a microphone in hand to sing? You must be kidding. Me lay hands on the sick? I'm too shy. Me witness for Jesus? I'll pray for laborers instead. Me go on a missions trip? I'm afraid of flying or water or spiders. I don't have time. I don't have money.*

Hello? What are you saying? God has called you to walk in abundant life and that means you walk right past the natural course on into the supernatural course. God has not given you a spirit of fear (2 Timothy 1:7). God said He will supply all your need (Philippians 4:19). Jesus said He always did those things that pleased the Father (John 8:29). Bottom line, there are no good excuses not to do what God tells you to do.

We just plain need to get over ourselves so the Greater One can flow through us.

Trust me. I do lots of things these days I never dreamed I could do. When I was a teenager singing in a group in my parents' church, I shook badly standing in front of people. I remember a time I was so frightened I held on to the girl next to me to keep from falling down. But I'm here to testify that when you move past your own human inabilities, you step into God's abilities. When you're no longer enough, He's more than enough. That's what divine life will do for you. That's when you begin living beyond the ordinary. That's when you begin doing and succeeding at things you never thought possible.

ACTION ▷ ···

Take an honest inventory of yourself and face a fear or an attitude or a harsh self-opinion that's held you back and write it below. Now do something about it! Get God's Word on the inside of you *and* boldly face that fear. Put fear in its proper place—under your feet. Begin taking bold steps for God today, and by tomorrow you'll walk in a whole new place.

WHAT FEAR SAYS	WHAT GOD SAYS	WHAT YOU'RE DOING ABOUT IT!

⑥ | CHEESE ON YOUR NOSE

Have you heard the story about the man napping with cheese on his nose? As the story goes, a few kids sneaked into a room where a man was sleeping on a couch and put a piece of Limburger cheese on his mustache. If you're not familiar with that particular cheese, let me explain that it has a *strong* odor. Actually, it stinks! So pretty soon the sleepy man began to wake up smelling something stinky and unpleasant. Finally, he woke up, jumped up and said, "Whew! It *really stinks* in here!"

He ran to the kitchen looking for the source of the problem and thought, *It stinks in here, too! He* went to the bedroom sniffing and thought, *Oh, man, it stinks in here, too! I'm getting out of this house.* Finally he opened the front door and walked outside. *Sniff. Sniff.*

"Whoa, it stinks out here, too," he said. "It's terrible, but I guess the whole world stinks!"

Guess what? The real problem was right under his nose.

Likewise, we often think, *If God would just change my spouse. If God would just change my boss or my kids or my mother-in-law or my roommate or whomever.* Some folks are always looking for God to change something else or someone else when the real change that's needed is in you and me. Have you ever noticed that whenever we desire change in any situation, God begins the change *in us.* God's style is always to start with us, working from the inside out.

The first step to fixing a problem is to recognize there is a problem. Think of an area of life where you really want change. Now get honest with God. Ask Him how you're part of the problem and how you can be part of the solution. Ask the Spirit of God to flood your heart and mind with light (Ephesians 1). That's His job, and He's good at it.

(7) | PASSIONATE PURSUIT

Awhile back I was meditating on the importance of worship in our lives, and I decided to look up the meaning of the word in The American Heritage Dictionary. I discovered the word *worship* means *to love and pursue devotedly.* I love that definition and believe it perfectly describes *how* we are to worship God.

Actually, it reminds me of how my husband, Mark, pursued me before we were married. I'm so glad he did. At the time I was traveling with the late Kenneth E. Hagin's singing group called Faith's Creation going one direction, and Mark was working for the same ministry traveling another direction. Rarely did our paths cross. When they did, we would go out to dinner as really good friends. That was all I could ever see us being because we never had enough time together to really get to know each other.

Finally, I told Mark, "I enjoy being with you. You're a great friend. But I don't really know you, and the only way we would get to know each other is to have more time together. You and I both know that would take a miracle because I'm going one way and you're going another way."

But before long, Mark had a habit of just showing up in Brother Hagin's meetings around the country. Our group would be singing, and I would look out to see Mark Brazee in the audience. *Hmmm! What's he doing here?* I wondered.

After the service I would ask him, "What are you doing here? I thought you were in such-and-such a place."

"Oh, I was just in the area," he would say.

Come to find out, he drove like a thousand miles nonstop to get to those meetings because he was pursuing me, and it paid off. He won my heart. The point is, we need to pursue the presence of God the same way —*passionately.* We need to pursue God in order to develop our relationship with Him. We need to get comfortable in His presence, and we need to get to know Him intimately.

The apostle Paul said, "[For my determined purpose is] that I may know Him [that I may progressively become more deeply and intimately acquainted with Him, perceiving and recognizing and understanding the wonders of His Person more strongly and more clearly], and that I may in that same way come to know the power outflowing from His resurrection..." (Philippians 3:10 AMP).

God has a wonderful personality, and we can come to know Him well. How? There are many ways, but they all come down to one thing: T I M E. Think about it. Time together is how you got to know your best friend on the earth. Time together is how I got to know Mark, and it's how we all get to know God. As we spend time with God, we can know Him through praise and worship, through His Word, through prayer, through service to Him and in so many ways. Eventually our time with Him will show. We'll be on fire—ablaze—for all the world to see.

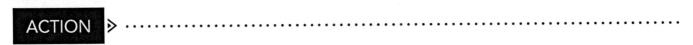

ACTION ▷

Don't make time for everything else and then try to figure out where to squeeze in God. Make time for God and let everything else fit around Him. Get out your calendar and schedule a date with God.

(8) | ALL-CONSUMING WORSHIP

Worship is much more than slow, quiet music that follows praise in our church services. *Worship* means we offer God our love, our adoration, our time, our service—ourselves. Our worship to Him must be all-consuming and with no limitations. It doesn't matter what anyone else thinks; all that matters is what God thinks. We are to be in passionate pursuit of Him—*knowing Him more, loving Him more and serving Him more.*

Our goal should be to please God in everything we do. We can never afford to think, *Aw, not now. I don't feel like worshipping.* No, worship needs to be an on-purpose, passionate pursuit of His presence. It's how we keep ourselves ignited and on fire for God.

Everything about your life for the Lord should be fervent. In fact, Paul said to be "fervent in spirit; serving the Lord" (Romans 12:11 KJV). The Amplified Bible says, "Never lag in zeal *and* in earnest endeavor; be aglow and burning with the Spirit...." The Message translation says, "Don't burn out; keep yourselves fueled and aflame...." Janet's translation says, "Never let your worship be flippant; let it always be fervent. Never allow yourself to be cool or casual. Never allow yourself to live half-heartedly before God or do only enough to get by."

Be on fire for God. Let your very life worship God passionately from morning to night every day of your life in everything you do. The American Heritage Dictionary describes the word *passionate* this way: *a powerful, boundless emotion; an abandoned display of emotion.* Let these words soak in. Powerful. Boundless. An abandoned display. Settle for nothing less than passionate worship. Whether in a church service or in your quiet place at home. Tune out the world and focus on Him. Give yourself wholly to Him. Hold nothing back. And no matter how long or how well you've known Him, passionately pursue Him even more.

ACTION ▷ ....

As you go throughout your day, whisper words of love and worship to the Lord no matter what you're doing. He will love hearing from you, and it will remind you to passionately worship Him with your life.

⑨ | PRAISE YOUR WAY OUT

In Acts 16 we read about two preachers who were having a very bad day. Paul and Silas had gotten arrested for preaching the gospel and landed in jail. What did they do about it? Did they have a pity party? Did they complain? They had plenty of opportunity to cry and feel sorry for themselves as they sat bound and chained in a dirty jail.

But the Bible says at midnight—when things looked the worst—they praised the Lord so loudly that the other prisoners heard them. Obviously Paul and Silas were not whispering quietly under their breath. They praised God loudly and boldly, and they didn't care who heard them. Everyone heard them. Even God heard them, and then something happened.

The earth began to quake. The jail began to shake, and their chains fell off. Paul and Silas were set free by the power of God.

Do circumstances or thoughts or symptoms have you feeling like you're bound in jail? Do you feel trapped? Then it's time to praise your way out. Open your mouth, turn up the volume and begin to praise the same BIG GOD they praised. In your darkest midnight hour, praise God. Praise Him loud and praise Him long.

ACTION ▷ ....

Lift your voice and tell Him now: *You are good and Your mercy endures forever and ever. Pain goes as I lift my voice. Fear goes as I lift my voice. Thoughts go as I lift my voice. Jesus set me free so I am free!*

I'm free!

I'm free!

What God did for Paul, He'll do for me. If You did it once, You'll do it twice. I choose to live a life of worship. I choose to live a life of praise. I choose to live a life of victory.

(10) | CREATING AN ATMOSPHERE

It's interesting how we create an atmosphere around us wherever we are. We create the atmosphere in our homes, whether it's one of peace or strife, and we do it with our words or the music we're playing or the television show we're watching. We also create atmospheres in church services. Through our praise and worship, we create an atmosphere where God is at home or not at home.

Psalm 22:3 says God lives and dwells in the praises of His people, and what an honor it is when we praise Him that He comes in manifested presence. Of course, the Spirit of God lives inside every born-again Christian. The Bible says He will never leave us or forsake us. If we're born again, He is inside of us whether we feel like He is or not. Yet, when we talk of experiencing His manifested presence, we talk of recognizing and sensing Him tangibly in our lives, homes and services.

One of the most important things we can do to enjoy this manifested presence is nothing—nothing at all. When we gather in church and begin to praise and worship, we need to leave all the busyness of life and our thoughts about jobs, relationships and everything else out in the car. When we're at home praising and worshipping God, we need to leave the cares of home in the other room. We need to leave anything and everything behind. Whatever happened today, God can help us figure out tomorrow. When we worship, God must be our sole focus. As we give ourselves to Him completely, our worship bypasses our minds and lets our spirits fellowship intimately with the Father. Amazingly enough, we often come away with the very answer we needed in the first place.

ACTION ▷ ···

Turn off everything else in your mind right now and begin to talk to your Father about His goodness, His faithfulness, His mercy, His grace and His great love for you. Give yourself to Him completely. Then, out of a heart full of worship, thankfully tell Him all the ways His goodness and mercy are evident in your life.

⑪ | COME CLOSER

Distance is usually what keeps us from hearing the direction we need in life. This became clear to me recently as I walked down the hallway in my own home. Walking from a back bedroom toward the family room, I could hear a male voice I didn't recognize. At first I thought Mark was watching someone on television who was talking, but as I got closer, I realized it was Mark's voice after all. By the time I rounded the corner to enter the family room, I could hear every word Mark was saying.

Let that soak in for a minute because that's also how we hear from God. We can be walking along in life wanting—even desperately needing—to hear from God, but we're not close enough to recognize His voice or understand His words. We might even recognize He's speaking something to us, but the words or the message is just not clear.

In those times, you need to move in closer. You need to worship. Worship gets you in the room with God. Worship gets you close enough to hear what He's saying – no more wondering, trying to interpret or guess what He's saying. Worship brings you face to face with the One who has all the answers.

We need to get out of the back bedroom, so to speak. We need to get out of the hallway. If we get in the room where God is speaking, we'll get the direction we need.

ACTION ▷ ···

Read over these scriptures in a few different Bible translations, and write down what the Holy Ghost quickens to your heart about them. Then move in closer.

Romans 8:14 _____

1 Corinthians 2:9-12_____

Jeremiah 33:3_____

(12) | WAKE-UP CALL

God desires for you to be filled with His presence from the top of your head to the soles of your feet. Fingertip-to-fingertip and wall-to-wall, God wants you filled with Him, and He wants His presence flowing out from the core of *you*. Yet far too many Christians walk around with the short end of the spiritual stick even though it isn't at all God's plan. Too often believers subconsciously think that being full of God must be for someone else who is super spiritual. But God wants every one of us filled up with Himself.

Instead of walking short on His presence, you need to be "...filled [through all your being] unto all the fullness of God [may have the richest measure of the divine Presence, and become a body wholly filled and flooded with God Himself]" (Ephesians 3:19 Amp). You should overflow on people everywhere you go. Every one of us should be so full of God that He oozes out of us daily.

We should be filled to spill.

The apostle Paul told the born-again, Spirit-filled believers at Ephesus, "Be not drunk with wine wherein there is excess, but *be filled with the Spirit...*" (Ephesians 5:18 KJV). The literal Greek says *be being filled*, which is present tense. So did Paul mean believers should get filled with the Holy Ghost and relax for the rest of their lives? No. He told them to be filled—keep being filled—and do whatever it takes to stay filled.

The Bible tells us the same thing today. That's why even in this hour God is sending out a wake-up call to His Church. The truth is, if you want God's best in your life, you will have to give God your best. That starts with getting full, and that starts right now.

ACTION ≫ ·

Let me encourage you to pray in the Spirit (Acts 2, Jude 20). It will build you up and fill you up. "How will I know when I'm filled to the full?" You'll know and so will everyone around you.

⑬ | HUNGRY FOR MORE

Don't be drunk with wine, because that will ruin your life.
Instead, be filled with the Holy Spirit.
Ephesians 5:18 NLT

When God tells us in Ephesians 5 to be filled with the Spirit, He sure didn't mean "a little dab will do ya." It's not an instruction to seek a goose-bump touch from God once in a while. It's not only praying in the Spirit on special occasions or in moments of crisis. No, this scripture is talking about a lifestyle of being filled to the brim and overflowing with the Spirit of God on a day-to-day basis.

Jesus said in Matthew 5:6, "Blessed are they which do hunger and thirst after righteousness: for they shall be filled" (KJV). No wonder this is true. Whatever we have an appetite for is what we'll be filled with, so if we hunger and thirst for more of God, then more of God will fill us.

Quite honestly, sometimes you must retrain your appetite to be hungry for the right foods. You retrain your natural appetite to eat vegetables and salads instead of cookies and more cookies. Likewise, sometimes you must retrain your spiritual appetite to be hungry for God. If you're not hungry for more of God, be honest about it. You're not hopeless. In fact, if you admit your lack of hunger, you're on your way to changing your appetite.

How do you retrain your appetite to be hungry for the things of God? Sow your time toward spiritual things and you will reap spiritual growth. Galatians 5:16, says, "...Walk in the Spirit, and you shall not fulfill the lust of the flesh." *Ouch,* you might think, *walking in the Spirit sounds like a pipe dream too big to attain.* But it is *possible* to walk in the Spirit because God would not instruct you to do something that was not possible. Decide now that God's Word is true. You can do it!

ACTION ≫ ···

Now it's time to practice what was preached. Spend time sowing to the spirit. Devour the Word. Pray. Listen to anointed Christian music. Worship. Meditate. And don't stop short. You fill yourself with food until hunger pangs go away; now fill yourself with the Word and the Spirit until you're just as satisfied. Take a few minutes to jot down just how satisfying it is to be full of the Word and the Spirit.

_____

_____

_____

_____

_____

_____

_____

(14) | TRAPS AND TEMPTATIONS

Don't think it's strange if things in this world tug at you and tempt you. After all, the devil's job is to set traps and toss temptations your way. But you can win! There is always a solution and a way of escape. First Corinthians 10:13 says, "…God is faithful, who will not allow you to be tempted beyond what you are able, but with the temptation will also make the way of escape, that you may be able to bear it."

I like what early 20th century apostle of faith Smith Wigglesworth said, "If we live in the spirit, we shall find that all that is carnal is swallowed up in life."* The life of God will swallow up anything and everything carnal in our life. But let me tell you something important: God doesn't decide if you will be full of the Spirit. You do.

It's totally and completely up to *you*.

The truth is, whatever you focus on the most will fill you, and whatever fills you the most will flow out of you.

Unfortunately, a lot of people aren't focused on God, so He isn't able to fill them. They need one of those wake-up calls that we talked about earlier. They've lost their zeal, which The Nelson's New Illustrated Bible Dictionary defines as *enthusiastic devotion, eager desire and single-minded allegiance*. Face facts. Too many in the Church have become zealous in the wrong direction. Too many Christians aren't all that concerned about sin these days. Adultery is a piece of cake in the minds of some. *So and so couldn't help him or herself*, they reason. Are you kidding me? Sin is sin, folks. God has not changed; sin has not either. God is very explicit about it in His Word, and He says those who sin will not inherit the kingdom of God (1 Corinthians 6:9). That's pretty straight forward.

The good news is that if you walk in the Spirit, you don't have to be concerned with the lusts of the flesh. If you're tempted in an area, remember that the fuller you get of God, the less the world will be able to pull on you. Someone might say, "But I just can't help myself." Oh, yes, you can! And God will help you, too. God plans to fill you up with Himself so things of the world drop off. In fact, the world can't hold a candle to the excitement of the Creator of the universe living inside you.

ACTION ▷ ....

Step # 1: The most important step to overcoming temptation is to admit the temptation to yourself.

Step # 2: Decide to walk in victory.

Step #3: Get full of the Word and full of the Spirit.

Step #4: Watch the temptation fall away.

*Smith Wigglesworth: *Experiencing God's Power Today*, Whitaker House, Kensington, PA., 2000.

15 | GET IN, OUT OR RUN OVER

We're living in the last of the last days, and there's a great harvest of souls that must be won. Yet, we can only accomplish the work of the end-time harvest by doing the works of Jesus, which requires us to be full of God and fervent. We sure won't get it done in a passive, apathetic state.

God feels strongly about the temperature of believers. In fact, the word *fervent* means *to be hot and boil*. Take note! Jesus said, "I know thy works, that thou art neither cold nor hot…. So then because thou art lukewarm…I will spue thee out of my mouth" (Revelation 3:15-16 KJV). God doesn't want lukewarm Christians who are half in and half out of His plans and purposes. Actually, as the old song says, get in, get out or get run over.

That may sound harsh, but too many folks think, *If it's convenient, I'll go to church today. If it's convenient, I'll pray today. If I've got time, I'll read my Bible before I fall asleep.* It's actually been surveyed that the average Christian attends church only 2.5 times per month. That would mean if a pastor wanted to preach a message to his or her whole congregation, he would have to repeat it four weeks in a row so they all could hear it. Something is wrong with that picture.

For too many Christians, God has become a matter of convenience, but that's not what fervency and zeal are all about. "Never be lacking in zeal, but keep your spiritual fervor, serving the Lord" (Romans 12:11 NIV). The Voice translation says, "Let your spirit be on fire, bubbling up and boiling over, as you serve the Lord." God wants us on fire, fervent, hot, bubbling up and boiling over with the things of the Spirit.

We can either live on a lower plane where the lusts of the flesh control and dominate us, or we can rise up higher where God leads us and guides us. God wants us fervent and zealous for Him. He wants us filled with all that He is and all that He has.

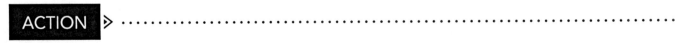

ACTION ≫ ···

Here's a Holy Ghost psalm that came up in my heart. Read it a few times, and then by faith speak out a psalm the Holy Ghost gives *you*.

Be filled with zeal. Be fervent with fire. Walk in the Spirit and you'll fulfill His desire.

All that is of the flesh will be burned to ash as we encounter His power reserved for this hour.

So rise up. Make a decision. Make a choice. Run your race and obey His voice.

Filled with zeal and fervent with fire, be determined to live a whole lot higher.

(16) | ALL TIMES

I will bless the Lord at all times: his praise shall continually be in my mouth.
Psalm 34:1 KJV

Did you notice the psalmist David did not say, "I will bless the Lord when I feel like it." He also did not say, "I will bless the Lord when it's a good day and everything goes my way." No. David said, "I will bless the Lord at *all times*." How many times is *all times*? It's every single one. That means we bless the Lord in good times, bad times and ugly times.

David went on to say, "His praise *shall* continually be in my mouth." *Shall* means *will*. Period. No doubt about it. No fail. In other words, you must choose to praise God. It's not a feeling; it's a decision. No matter what comes your way today, will you be in the mulligrubs or will you bless the Lord?

Most Christians have noticed it's easy to bless the Lord in church, but what about when you're not in church? What about when thoughts bombard your mind in the middle of the night and you wonder, *What will I do? How will I make it? What if the money doesn't come? What if the doctor gives me a bad report? What's the solution to this mess I'm facing?* That's when you must decide to praise God. These are some of the "all times" David was talking about.

It's great to praise and worship God in a corporate setting; I'm so thankful for it. It gives you a boost you need. But God's tangible presence also can fill your home in the middle of the night or your car in the middle of the day. When you bless the Lord at all times, He can surround you wherever you are with His manifested presence, and in Him is every kind of help or answer you need.

ACTION ▷ ···

Spend time reading and meditating on these scriptures. It will do you a world of good!

Psalm 138:8 | 1 Thessalonians 5:18 | 1 Corinthians 15:57

⑰ | MAGNIFY THE LORD

Oh, magnify the Lord with me, and let us exalt His name together.
Psalm 34:3

When I put on my reading glasses, letters and words on a page are magnified so I can comfortably read them, but do the letters and words really change? No. Glasses don't change the actual size of the letters at all. They act as a magnifying glass to magnify our vision. Nothing is really different, but we see differently. In the same way, when we magnify the Lord during hard times, He becomes bigger in our eyes than the problem we're facing.

Our focus should be on God, not on what's going on around us. Our focus should be on what God says about the problem because what God says *actually can change* what we're facing. But as long as we're focused on circumstances or situations or thoughts or imaginations or symptoms—or even other people's opinions—nothing will change for the better.

Second Corinthians 4:18 says, "While we do not look at the things which are seen, but at the things which are not seen. For the things which are seen are temporary, but the things which are not seen are eternal." In other words, every problem that comes our way is subject to change. It's subject to the name of Jesus. It's subject to the Word of God. "…This is the victory that has overcome the world—our faith" (1 John 5:4).

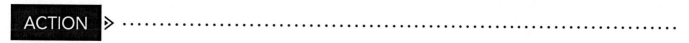

ACTION ▷ ....

The psalmist said, "Oh, magnify the Lord with me." I'm also encouraging you to magnify the Lord. Put on your spiritual eyeglasses and focus on Him. Magnify Him above whatever troubles are facing you. Begin to say: *Father, You're bigger! Your Word says greater are You in me than he that's in the world (1 John 4:4). I can do all things through Jesus Christ who strengthens me (Philippians 4:13). You meet all my need according to your riches in glory by Christ Jesus (Philippians 4:19). I can count on You because You never lie (Numbers 23:19).*

18 | RADIATE JESUS

I've always loved reading Acts 4:13 where people could tell the apostles had been with Jesus. I'm sure they had a glow about them because a person's countenance tells all. When people have been with Jesus, they radiate Him. They look like Him, act like Him and sound like Him. Actually, there's nothing super spiritual or complicated about radiating Jesus. It simply comes from spending time in His presence and hanging out with Him.

James 4:8 invites us to draw near to Him and promises in return that He will draw near to us. We become His vessels or agents. We become His hands, His mouth and His feet on this earth. The Bible sums it up by saying "…as He is, so are we in this world" (1 John 4:17).

The whole point is that the presence of God is not reserved for your church or your prayer closet. It's also to be experienced in your living room, your bedroom, your automobile, your kitchen, your job and everywhere else you go. There should be no place we would rather be than in the presence of God, and there's no place He would rather we be. His presence changes us from the inside out, and that's good enough for me.

Moses spent 40 days in the presence of God on top of a mountain, and it changed him. When he came down, his face glowed (Exodus 34:35). It was clear in Acts 4 that Peter and John had spent time with Jesus, which is God's plan. It's how He intends for us to portray Jesus to the world.

"Well, if I'm a Christian, don't I automatically portray Jesus?" No, it doesn't automatically happen. Radiating Jesus comes from spending time in His presence. I've heard about couples married 40 and 50 years who begin to look alike. Actually, it's no wonder because they have lived together so long, sharing the same experiences, climates, foods and more. If you've been around a couple like this, you'll notice they finish each other's sentences. They tell the same stories and use the same hand gestures because they've hung around together so long it shows.

In the same way, I believe the tangible presence of God can be seen on our faces as we leave the presence of God and enter our jobs, our schools, even our grocery stores. I believe the tangible presence of God can be so radiant upon us that people look at us and wonder, *What's different about that man or woman? There's just something special about that person.* You and I will know that something special we're radiating is Jesus Himself.

ACTION ▷ ....

You've got a good start already today but continue spending time in the presence of God. Hang out with Him. Read and meditate the Word. Write down what He speaks to your heart. Pray. Then watch how His tangible presence will change your very countenance.

_____

_____

_____

_____

_____

_____

_____

⑲ | TURN ON THE LIGHTS

On a flight coming home to Tulsa, a young woman sat next to me who traveled to Haiti for a week helping a medical missions team. It was amazing to hear the stories she told. She talked about how the nation was still in great turmoil and devastation years after a major earthquake in 2010. She told about problems obtaining clean drinking water, food, medical help, housing and more. She said the people needed help in so many areas.

One comment she made particularly captured my attention. She said the country only enjoyed a few hours of electricity each day, never knowing when the lights would turn on—morning, noon or night. Worse yet, she said the nation was dark spiritually with voodoo and satanic worship prevalent in many areas. I was amazed by how much darkness could exist in this small country only one hour from our United States' coastline where the light shines so bright.

I believe we have an obligation to pray for Haiti and all the nations of the world so that the eyes of their understanding would be flooded with light (Ephesians 1). When spiritual light comes, natural light will follow. When the Good News of Jesus comes, the lights are turned on in so many ways. As the body of Christ, it's our responsibility to pray for all the nations of the world to receive the light of the glorious gospel of Jesus Christ. Not a day should go by that we don't pray for nations of the world.

Consider this. If a room was pitch black, how many lights would it take to dispel the darkness? Just one. One light, whether it's a small candle in the corner or a big spotlight in the center, will eliminate darkness.

Never should we take for granted the light in our own country. Never should we take for granted the name of Jesus. We're a blessed people. We can turn on the television and radio, and the light of the gospel comes rushing through those signals. We can attend church. We can carry our Bibles. We can speak and worship freely. Yet, it's not that way all over the world. It's not even that way one hour from Miami.

I challenge you to pray that the light invades darkness wherever darkness is found—around our neighborhoods, around our cities, around our nation and around the world. We need to be ever thankful and grateful for the light we have, but we cannot afford to be selfish with it. We must do our part to spread the light that Jesus is alive, and He's the same yesterday, today and forever.

ACTION ▷ ·

What nation comes up in your heart? I commit to pray for _____.
On a regular basis, I will pray for its people and its leaders to be flooded with the light of the glorious gospel.

20 | RUN TO HIM

Awhile back our three-year-old great niece came to spend the night at our home. When my nephew's vehicle pulled up, I saw the car through my kitchen window and began walking toward the front door. I could see that he was unbuckling her car seat, so I opened the front door just in time to see Kaylee running toward me as fast as her little legs could carry her down the sidewalk. I bent down with my arms wide open and said, "Come on, Kaylee! Come on!" She ran and grabbed me with the biggest hug ever. I'm telling you what. That child could have asked for the moon, and I would have figured out a way to get it for her. She absolutely melted my heart.

With big blue eyes, she would look at me throughout the evening and say, "Aunt Janet, I love you!" Each time my heart would melt all over again. It meant the world to me when she expressed her love to me, and it means the world to God when we express our love to Him. I thought later about how we run into God's arms just the way my great niece ran into mine.

We welcome God through our praise, and we love Him through our worship. We throw the door open and say, "God, we welcome you in this place. We welcome you in our lives. It's not about us; it's about You." Then He opens His arms wide for us to run into a place of safety, peace and joy. We run into a place where we can take hold of anything we need because He has everything we need. He's El Shaddai, which in Hebrew means *the God who is more than enough*. That's our God. He has the answer to every question and the solution to every problem. He's all we'll ever need.

More than anything, He is worthy of our praise just because of who He is. The visit with Kaylee gave me a much better understanding of the Father's love toward us. When we enter His presence, we need to take the time to communicate our love to Him. If it does a fraction of what "I love you, Aunt Janet!" did to me, it will go a long, long way.

Never back off from the presence of God. Don't back off because you're too busy, because you've sinned and feel guilty, because you're tired or because of any other reason. In fact, run to Him. Tell Him, "Father, I'm running into Your arms because I love You with all that's in me."

ACTION ▷ ···

Run into His arms now. There's no better time. Afterward, take a few moments to share how His love and His presence changed you. You'll want to go back and read it again from time to time.

_____

_____

_____

_____

_____

_____

㉑ | SPREAD LIKE WILDFIRE

As a little girl growing up in Florida, my family didn't enjoy fires too often, but every now and then, we cozied up in front of a warm and toasty fire. I loved watching my daddy build a fire the old-fashioned way. We didn't have fancy gas logs, so he would bend down and roll newspapers to wedge between logs in the hearth. Daddy would strike a match and light the newspapers until a little flame would appear. Woosh! Then down on his hands and knees, Daddy would blow. Wooo! Wooo! Before long, a flame danced through the logs until a roaring fire ignited that could be felt across the room.

In the same way, the wind of the Holy Ghost blows on our lives and ignites the fire of God in us. Let's fan the Holy Ghost fire in us. Let's stoke the coals. Let's spread like wildfire and take our filled-up and fired-up selves to the world.

When the fire of God comes on you, you won't be able to sit quietly and meditate about God. Of course it's easy to sit in your chair unaffected and unemotional when you're not on fire, but when you're on fire, you cannot sit still. You cannot be quiet, and you don't care who knows it because it's like fire shut up in your bones (Jeremiah 20:9).

The fire of God will fill you up, turn you around, and send you out to a world that's waiting on *you*. So keep yourself stirred up and keep your fire burning hot. "How?" somebody might ask. Spend time in God's Word. Pray. Praise. Worship. Go to church. Hang around with other filled-up and fired-up believers and keep the fire burning. In these days that we are living, we need the fire burning hotter, brighter and more fervent than ever.

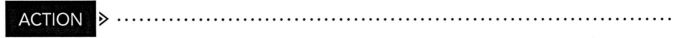

ACTION ▷ ···

There are people you need to reach. Don't just pray that laborers are sent across the paths of those you know and love, but ask God if *you are that laborer*. Either way, it's always right to love on people, so go spread some wildfire for God!

(22) | YOUR PRESENCE IS HEAVEN TO ME

In their mid-to-late 80s, my parents lived in a memory care facility with about a dozen or so other people nearby them. Most of the time when I would visit them, I would walk in to see them sitting side by side with big smiles on their faces. The staff at the facility and even other visitors would tell me my parents glowed. It was true. I could see it myself.

The head nurse asked me one day, "That glow on them is the joy of the Lord, isn't it?"

"Yes, it is!" I said.

The same nurse called me into her office another visit and said, "I was just talking about you and telling another nurse how you were here recently singing to your parents. I told her how your momma lifted up her hands and worshipped with tears flowing down her cheeks. The amazing thing is how that could happen even though her memory capacity doesn't really function. I'm not sure I really even understand, but the minute you began to sing, she began to worship. It's like the worship flowed out of her heart and bypassed her mind altogether."

"That's exactly what happens!" I told the nurse. "It's pretty supernatural, isn't it?"

That's what happens to all of us when we worship from our hearts. Our worship bypasses our minds, and our spirits communicate with God. Jesus Himself explained, "God is Spirit, and those who worship Him must worship in spirit and truth," (John 4:24). What a wonderful thing to worship and fellowship with God spirit to spirit. We're not limited by our minds, our knowledge, our vocabulary, our thoughts, our circumstances or anything else. No matter what we're dealing with or what's going on around us, we can bypass it all by tapping into the presence of God.

So often after we worship, we just know on the inside the answer or direction we needed. As we give ourselves to God in worship, He imparts Himself to us, and in Him is anything and everything we need.

There are times in life when you may feel like peace and joy are nowhere to be found. But as you worship and enter the presence of God, peace and joy will well up from within and rest on you. It will be evident to you and all those around you. Don't leave home without the presence of God. In fact, don't live without it.

ACTION ▷ ···

Turn on some anointed music and bask in the presence of God.

(23) | LIFE JACKET

Have you ever felt like you're drowning in troubles? Maybe you feel like you're going under for the last time? You're not alone. God has a life jacket for you called the Word of God and just one word is enough to pull you out of trouble. If you're facing some winds and waves in this life, grab hold.

"That's not fair! If Peter had a Bible, then he could have walked on water," someone might say. First of all, Peter did have God's Word, and He did walk on water (Matthew 14). Jesus said "Come!" and every step Peter took, he took on that Word of God. Think about it! It only took one word from heaven for Peter to do the impossible.

Then Peter threw the one word overboard. He got his eyes off Jesus and the Word and on the winds and waves. Peter began to focus on symptoms, circumstances and situations around him instead of focusing on Jesus. *Then* he began to sink.

Peter got consumed with the problem, and he got consumed with water. Yet, even after Peter's so-called faith failure, Jesus didn't say, "Peter, you unspiritual idiot! Just sink!" No. Jesus reached out His hand, pulled Peter on top of the water and probably shared a faith lesson with him on the way back to the boat. Jesus came to Peter's rescue just like Jesus will come to yours. I'm sure Jesus told Peter, "Keep your eyes on Me, and you won't sink. Forget the wind and the waves. Trust Me. You stepped out on My Word, so continue on My Word. I would never lead you where I cannot protect and provide for you."

Jesus is saying the same thing to us. Just trust Me! Get your eyes off the problem and look to Me, the Author and Finisher of your faith.

Pour out your praise on Him *until you recognize* that He is greater than any problem. Begin to say: *Problem? What problem? Jesus, You are bigger than the problem. My focus is on You. Thank You that You are the way, the truth and the life. You're my way out of this situation. You make a way where there is no way. You never leave me or forsake me. And You always come to my rescue.*

ACTION ▷ ··

Sometimes the best way to get a life jacket for yourself is to throw a life jacket to another person who needs one. Think of one person today who's facing a situation even more challenging than yours and build them up with faith and love.

㉔ | GIVING THANKS

In everything give thanks; for this is the will of God in Christ Jesus for you.
1 Thessalonians 5:18

The Bible tells us to give thanks *in* everything, but it sure doesn't say we should give thanks *for* everything. Some people don't recognize there's a difference. Others get confused about the difference saying, "The Bible says we should give thanks *for* everything that comes along in life—the good, the bad, the ugly." No, that's not true. God doesn't want you to thank Him for something He didn't do or wouldn't do.

Jesus Himself was pretty clear on the topic in John 10:10 when he said, "The thief [the devil] does not come except to steal, and to kill, and to destroy. I have come that they may have life, and that they may have it more abundantly." That's as black and white as it gets. God wears the white hat. The devil wears the black hat. If it's good, it's from God. If it's bad, it's from the devil.

Let me put it this way. If something steals your health, money or peace of mind, it's the devil. God sure doesn't want you to thank Him for trouble the devil sends your way. God sent Jesus to destroy the works of the devil (1 John 3:8), and now He wants His children to live by faith (Hebrews 10:38) and be victorious (1 John 5:4). God wants you to use your faith to get rid of problems. James 1:17 says, "Every good gift and every perfect gift is from above, and comes down from the Father of lights, with whom there is no variation or shadow of turning."

"Well, those are great scriptures, but something doesn't make sense. If we don't give thanks *for* everything, why do we give thanks *in* everything?" It makes perfect sense. We give thanks in everything because we're giving thanks all the way through whatever it is until we pop out victorious on the other side of trouble. Romans 8:37 says you're more than a conqueror. You're not a survivor; you're an overcomer. But the truth is, in order for you to be an overcomer, you will have problems to overcome now and then. Nevertheless, you win! Read the back of The Book. It says we overcome by the blood of the lamb and the word of our testimony (Revelation 12:11).

Colossians 2:15 says Jesus stripped the devil of His power and authority. So take hold of the exceedingly great and precious promises of God's Word (2 Peter 1:4) and walk in victory every single time.

ACTION ▷

Faith is an act, so act like the Word is true. Give thanks today *in* whatever your facing and act like the overcomer you are.

(25) | WHAT HAPPENS WHEN YOU PRAISE

…You are safe and secure from all your enemies;
you stop anyone who opposes you.
Psalm 8:2 GNT

Praising God is no small thing. It puts God to work in your circumstances. While we are magnifying God and pouring our love out on Him, God is busy stopping the enemy.

Our text above says God stops the enemy. The New King James version says God silences the enemy. The King James version says God *quiets or stills* the enemy. I like the picture I'm getting. God stops the enemy and shuts him up.

If you've been a Christian very long at all, I'm sure you've noticed that the one positive thing that can be said about the devil is that he's persistent. He persistently tells one lie after another because the Bible says there is no truth in Him (John 8:44). You can count on the fact that anything he says cannot be true because nothing he says ever lines up with the Word of God.

See him for what he is. The devil is a loud-mouthed troublemaker. His whole purpose is to get you to question God's Word so he can steal it from you. He wants to get you off course. First Peter 5:8 says the devil is like a roaring lion going about seeking whom he may devour. But the roaring lion gets stopped in his tracks when he hears the voice of a believer pouring out his or her love on the Father.

There's a lot of talk in this day and age about being proactive with our health, nutrition, finances and a host of other things, but the most important place to be proactive is in our praise. When we praise, we enable God to work in our behalf.

In 2 Chronicles 20, King Jehoshaphat was terrified by the enemy armies coming against him, so he went to God for guidance. God told him the battle was His – not theirs. So Jehoshaphat instructed the people to worship God. Notice what happened. Verse 22 says, "Now when they began to sing and to praise, *the LORD set ambushes* against the people of Ammon, Moab, and Mount Seir, who had come against Judah; and they were defeated." Not one single enemy survived. The people praised, and God did the rest. It will work just the same for you.

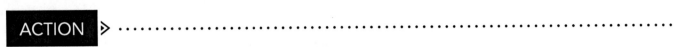

Fill in the chart with lies the devil tells you and the truth of God's Word that will combat it!

LIES THE DEVIL TELLS YOU	TRUTH GOD TELLS YOU

Praise God with the truth!

Praise! Praise! And praise some more!

Then just when you think you've praised enough, praise some more.

God will be busy stopping the enemy!

26 | ROPES COURSE

Trust in the LORD WITH ALL YOUR HEART, AND LEAN NOT ON YOUR OWN UNDERSTANDING;
In all your ways acknowledge Him, and He shall direct your paths.
Proverbs 3:5

So often we pray, "God, show me what to do. Show me where to go. Show me this. Show me that." But are we qualified to ask Him? Of course, God promises to direct our paths, but He also tells us to do something before direction will come. God tells us to trust Him, lean not to our own understanding and acknowledge Him in all our ways.

It all boils down to letting go and letting God.

I remember a time when our church staff decided to take a lesson in letting go and building trust in one another by attending a ropes course on the outskirts of Tulsa. Each staff member climbed up a platform in the air and on command fell backward to be caught by the rest of the staff on the ground. The staff formed two rows side-by-side and then faced each other linking arms to create a human net to catch the person. The whole point was for the falling person to *let go and trust* the team to catch him or her.

I was very polite and let everyone else go first. Actually, I was trying to find a way out of it, but finally they said, "You're up!" As I climbed the platform, I remember thinking, *This is the hardest thing I've ever done in my entire life. What if they don't catch me? What if I fall and go right through their arms? What if I get hurt? What if I land smack dab on the ground?"*

Have you ever been in a tight spot asking, *What if? What if God's Word doesn't hold me up? What if God doesn't come through for me? What if the medicine doesn't work? What if the money doesn't come? What if? What if? What if?*

Sure, we've all had thoughts like that. There's not a person alive who hasn't been afraid of something. I remember standing on that platform a long time thinking things over. Eventually it dawned on me, *There's no way out of this. If I don't do this, I'll be the only one, which would not be good. I have no choice but to trust the group."* So I took a deep breath, put my trust in God and fell.

That's how it is with the things of God; sometimes we just have to take a deep breath, trust God and let go. Usually we aren't able to see how things will turn out, but if we're trusting God we know it will all be good. God has only good plans for us. Jeremiah 29:11 says, "'For I know the plans I have for you,' says the LORD. 'They are plans for good and not for disaster, to give you a future and a hope'" (NLT).

Don't bother trying to figure out everything in life. You can't. It's a waste of time and energy. Instead, acknowledge God by saying, "I put my trust in You. I'm looking to You to get me through this. I'm looking to You to show me what to do and how to handle this situation. I need Your help because I can't fix it by myself. I put my life into Your hands. You're so much bigger and smarter! I trust You. I *trust You. I t-r-u-s-t You!*

ACTION ▷ ....

Admit to yourself and to God an area where you have trouble letting go. Actually, God already knows, but it will do you a world of good to confront it here.

What's the Word say about it?

_____

_____

_____

Now, take a deep breath. Let go and let God.

(27) | SING FOR JOY

Oh, let the nations be glad and sing for joy!
For You shall judge the people righteously,
And govern the nations on earth.
Psalm 67:4

When was the last time you heard a depressed person sing? The answer is never because depressed people do not sing. The truth is, no matter what challenges and troubles are facing you in life, there's a song in your heart that needs to be sung.

Whether or not you can technically hit the right notes is totally irrelevant. The Bible says over and over again through the book of Psalms to make a joyful noise (Psalm 66:1, Psalm 81:1, Psalm 95:1, Psalm 95:2, Psalm 98:4, Psalm 98:6 and Psalm 100:1). Your singing may be a noise to some, but that's all right because it's music to God's ears.

In fact, in the text above the psalmist said "…be glad and sing for joy!" Think about that. If you don't have joy, *sing for it!* In other words, sing until the joy comes. Make no mistake. If you sing to the Lord and elevate Him above the situations and circumstances you face, joy *will* come.

A while back, before my sweet, elderly momma stepped over to heaven, I was helping her eat her dinner in the memory care facility where she stayed. In between bites, she would sing. "Now, Momma," I began to joke with her, "you taught me never to sing at the table. You are eating dinner now." I began to laugh, and she did, too.

"Are you still singing?" I asked.

"Uh-huh," she said.

I thought about it for a minute and then said, "Well, Momma, you go ahead and sing all you want! You lift up your voice! You give God praise!" There was a song in her heart regardless of her situation, regardless of her circumstances. We should have that same song lifted up to Him.

The scripture says if we don't lift up our voice in praise and in worship, God will cause even the rocks to cry out (Luke 19:40). I don't know about you, but I don't want any rocks doing my praising for me.

ACTION ▷

Don't wait for another time or place. Lift your voice right now and sing to Him. Sing a song you know or sing a new song. Then lift up your hands and let Him fill your heart and your room with His presence. Begin to say to Him, *"I love You, dear Lord. I want to spend time with You. Thank You, Jesus, for all You've done. I am eternally grateful to You."*

(28) | USE WORDS IF YOU MUST

This people have I formed for myself; they shall shew forth my praise.
Isaiah 43:21 KJV

We were created to show forth God's praise and to show the world there is hope. We're to show the world how to walk in fellowship with God. Sometimes we will use words, and sometimes we won't.

I've heard it said, "Preach the Gospel at all times and when necessary use words." Yet, someone might ask, "How in the world do you preach the gospel if you don't use words?" The answer is this: Christians should preach the gospel with their lives.

The *zoe* life of God on the inside of us transforms us into the image of our Father and causes us to be a lighthouse to the world. Actually, the Bible says we are like lights set on a hill (Matthew 5:14), which means people should be drawn to us. There may be darkness all around, but people are drawn to light when it's dark. Jesus is the light of the world, and the Bible says as He is so are we in this world (1 John 4:17).

We should glow like the lightning bugs I used to chase in the dark when I was a kid. Actually, I still love to watch the glow and flicker of light against the darkness. May every one of us purpose to glow in the dark because of the light that dwells and lives in us. Let's shine for Him.

ACTION ▷ ....

DECLARE Jesus is the light of the world by declaring Jesus is the light in you. Say aloud: *Jesus is the light in me. I want the world to see Jesus in me. I choose to glow wherever I go. Jesus, use me. Shine through me. Demonstrate Yourself through me.* Then **SHINE** everywhere you go today. Purpose to radiate Jesus. Look people straight in the eye. Smile! Speak words that brighten the day of everyone you meet. Love on everyone you meet. Witness to everyone you meet and use words if you must.

(29) | LOVE IS LIKE AN OREO

Think of the Oreo cookie with its two chocolate cookie sides and creamy filling in the center. Now confess. When you eat an Oreo, do you take the cookie apart and eat the filling first or eat the whole cookie all together? Some people eat the cream filling first, which makes no sense to me because then you're left with two plain, dry chocolate cookies. In fact, then it's not even an Oreo anymore because it's the cream center that makes the Oreo the Oreo.

What's this have to do with anything important? Actually, the Holy Ghost talked to me about Oreo cookies recently. He did not tell me to eat more of them, but He did tell me how this cookie can help us understand the gifts of the Spirit. I've gone back and forth a lot between 1 Corinthians chapters 12 through 14 studying the gifts of the Spirit. Quite honestly, I've wondered many times why a chapter on love, 1 Corinthians 13, is stuck right smack dab in between two chapters on the gifts. I've thought, *Did Paul put that love chapter in the wrong place? Maybe he needed an editor to move it.* I like things organized; I like paragraphs to flow, so I couldn't understand why these two chapters on the gifts were interrupted by the love chapter.

The truth is, that chapter *is in exactly the right place*, and the Holy Ghost spoke to my heart explaining why: *"First Corinthians 12, 13 and 14 are like the Oreo cookie. Chapters 12 and 14 are the cookies, and chapter 13 is the creamy filling—or God's love—that holds them all together. Love keeps the gifts working right and puts divine order in their operation."*

The gifts of the Spirit are serious business, and we need them operating in our churches, out on the streets and in our lives. In fact, if there's one thing we need to start talking more about in this hour of the Church, it's the gifts of the Spirit. Smith Wigglesworth said this about the gifts: "Is there not a vast and an appalling unconcern about possessing the gifts? You may ask a score of believers—chosen at random, from almost any church–'Do you have any of the gifts of the Spirit?' The answer from all will be, 'No.' And it will be given in a tone and with a manner that conveys the thought that the believer is not surprised that he does not have the gifts, and that he doesn't expect to have any of them, and that he does not expect to seek them. Isn't this terrible, when the Living Word specifically exhorts us to earnestly desire the best gifts?"

Evidently that was the condition of the Church back in Rev. Wigglesworth's day. Yet amazingly enough, it sounds similar to the Church today. I grew up in a church my dad pastored where the primary gifts in manifestation on a regular and consistent basis were tongues and interpretation, although we don't see that so much in our churches today.

Let's change that! Let's earnestly desire the gifts as the Bible says. Let's talk more about the gifts so faith for them will rise. Let's learn more about the gifts so we can operate them. We need boldness to step out and flow in the gifts wherever we go. And, without a doubt, as we're filled with God's love the same way the Oreo center is filled with cream, God will use us in the gifts of the Spirit like never before.

ACTION ▷ ···

Spend some time reading and meditating 1 Corinthians 12, 13 and 14 and then note below what the Spirit of God has quickened to you about these chapters. And just maybe you should treat yourself to an Oreo…as an edible object lesson.

_____

_____

_____

_____

(30) | BANKRUPT WITHOUT LOVE

Love is not an option. God says we're bankrupt without it. In fact, look with me at what the Bible says about the God-kind of love: "If I speak with human eloquence and angelic ecstasy but don't love, I'm nothing but the creaking of a rusty gate. If I speak God's Word with power, revealing all his mysteries and making everything plain as day, and if I have faith that says to a mountain, 'Jump,' and it jumps, but I don't love, I'm nothing. If I give everything I own to the poor and even go to the stake to be burned as a martyr, but I don't love, I've gotten nowhere. So, no matter what I say, what I believe, and what I do, I'm bankrupt without love" (1 Corinthians 13:1-3 The Message).

Keep in mind that these scriptures aren't talking about the ooey–gooey kind of natural love based on feelings that go up and down like a yo-yo. Paul is talking about the God-kind of love "poured out in our hearts by the Holy Spirit…" (Romans 5:5). It's a supernatural love imparted the moment you're born again. You might say, "I'm born again, but I don't feel love in me." Nevertheless, if you're born again, God's love is in you whether you feel it or not, and it should dominate everything you do.

Let's continue in 1 Corinthians 13:4-8 in The Amplified Bible: "Love endures long *and* is patient and kind; love never is envious *nor* boils over with jealousy, is not boastful *or* vainglorious, does not display itself haughtily. It is not conceited (arrogant and inflated with pride); it is not rude (unmannerly) *and* does not act unbecomingly. Love (God's love in us) does not insist on its own rights *or* its own way, *for* it is not self-seeking; it is not touchy *or* fretful *or* resentful; it takes no account of the evil done to it [it pays no attention to a suffered wrong]. It does not rejoice at injustice *and* unrighteousness, but rejoices when right *and* truth prevail. Love bears up under anything *and* everything that comes, is ever ready to believe the best of every person, its hopes are fadeless under all circumstances, and it endures everything [without weakening]. Love never fails [never fades out or becomes obsolete or comes to an end]…."

These scriptures tell us exactly what God has deposited on the inside of every born-again Christian. Whether you feel like it or not, Romans 5:5 says the love of God was poured out in your heart. Choose to walk in love because it's a choice. Let God's love flow from you everywhere you go because I promise you this: To live *The God Life* and live beyond the ordinary, you must follow the God-kind of love. Without it, you're bankrupt. With it, you're overflowing with God Himself.

ACTION ▷ ....

Choose love today! In fact, try to keep track of just how many times you chose love today over any other response.

_____

_____

_____

_____

_____

_____

③1 | LOVE MADE EASY

There's an old saying that sticks and stones will break your bones, but words will never hurt you. That's just not true. Words can hurt deeply.

The truth is, our words are supposed to minister grace to the hearers and build up people. In plain old English, people should be better off because we've spoken. Unfortunately, I think a lot of times people would be better off if we would keep our mouths shut.

Ephesians 4:31-32 says, "Get rid of all bitterness, rage, anger, harsh words, and slander, as well as all types of evil behavior. Instead, be kind to each other, tenderhearted, forgiving one another, just as God through Christ has forgiven you" (NLT).

Since we're talking about words without malice and being tenderhearted, please note that love is not rudeness pretending to call itself boldness like some folks do. Our words need to be gentle and full of love.

Here are four words that will help you stay in love: *Not I, but Christ*. Galatians 2:20 actually says, "I am crucified with Christ: nevertheless I live; yet *not I, but Christ* liveth in me…" (KJV). Mediate on these words and keep them rolling around in your heart. These words will help you through life. Next time you wonder whether or not you should say something, these words will rise up and answer your question.

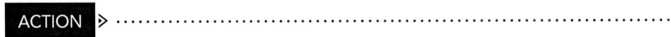

ACTION ▷ ....

Say these four important words over and over: *Not I, but Christ*. The more you say these four words, the easier time you'll have with the three important words: I love you.

(32) | FIT AND BUFF

…Bodily exercise profits a little, but godliness is profitable for all things, having promise of the life that now is and of that which is to come.

1 Timothy 4:8

Everywhere we look these days—the news, magazines, even social media—we're told how important it is to be physically fit. We're told that to live long and be healthy we need to eat right and exercise. It's true, of course. We only have one body, and we need to take good care of it. Yet, at the same time, we need to be spiritually fit. To be ready and stay ready for what God has called and trained us to do, we need to take good care of our spirits.

Colossians 3:16 gives us good advice about being fit spiritually, saying, "Let the word of Christ dwell in you richly…." The Janet translation says, "Be so full of God's Word that you're like a sponge full of water. Then, no matter how you're squeezed, the Word will come out!" The truth is, if we'll take the time to put God's Word in our spirits, it will show up in our lives. It will show up in our bodies and our minds. It will show up in our homes, families, relationships, churches and even on our jobs.

There's no question that Jesus was full of the Word. John 1:14 says Jesus *was* the Word made flesh, and He always pleased the Father (John 8:29). Jesus was the will of God in action, and the Word dictated His life. It also needs to dictate ours. Whatever the Word says is exactly how we should live. No discussion. No debate. No question.

To be spiritually fit we also need to be full of the Spirit. Acts 13:52 says the disciples were "were filled with joy and with the Holy Spirit," and as a result, the book of Acts was filled with signs, wonders and miracles. New Testament Christians weren't running on empty or running on fumes. No, they were continually *full* of joy and *full* of the Holy Spirit. We also need to get full. One great way to do that is to pray in tongues every single day. Don't use the excuse that you don't have time; make time. Pray on the way to work. Pray while you're in the shower. Pray while you're driving in the car. Just pray! (Janet Brazee teaches more on this topic in her book titled *TONGUES: Language of the Supernatural*.)

Finally, we need to exercise spiritually just as we exercise physically. There's no way around it. The Bible says the just shall live by faith, (Hebrews 10:38) which means we exercise our faith muscle. When problems or symptoms come against us, we need to push them away with our faith and overcome them. "This is the victory that has overcome the world—our faith" (1 John 5:4).

As he teaches, Mark often uses the example of a weight lifter. He or she doesn't build muscles just lying on a bench with weight after weight piled on. No, the weight lifter's muscles get stronger as he or she *pushes away and resists the weights*. In the same way, our faith muscle gets stronger as we use it to resist problems, symptoms or whatever else the devil throws at us. We should *always* exercise our faith to believe for something. After we've believed God to meet our needs, we can always believe for more money to give to missions, and we can always believe for souls and more souls.

ACTION ▷ ···

Lay out an action plan to increase your spiritual fitness. Set some goals for yourself in all three categories.

MY GOALS
Getting full and staying full of the Word --
Getting full and staying full of the Spirit --
Where I will exercise my faith --

③③ | TURNAROUND TIME 1

*Turnaround (turn e-round') n. The act of turning about and
facing or moving in the opposite direction.
The American Heritage Dictionary*

Have you found yourself walking through life on the wrong spiritual road? Maybe you feel like you're on a dead end road or your life hasn't been the picture of a victorious Christian living the Bible promises? Maybe sickness is having a heyday in your body or you need direction. Maybe your financial picture or your relationships aren't too rosy.

The good news is that God is ready to help you. But you can't keep walking that same old, same old road. Walking as you have been won't get you anywhere different. There's only one thing to do. *Turn around. Face and move in an opposite direction.* Head toward God, walking a different way on a much better road.

Acts 3:19 says in The Amplified Bible, "So repent (change your mind and purpose); *turn around* and return [to God], that your sins may be erased (blotted out, wiped clean), that times of refreshing (of recovering from the effects of heat, of reviving with fresh air) may come from the presence of the Lord." The presence of God can make all the difference.

Luke is telling you that the first step toward change is yours to take. He said "…(change your mind and purpose); turn around and return [to God]…." If you've been praying, "God, please turn things around for me," you're in for a long wait. I can tell you right now that you're stuck traveling the same road until you change your thinking. In fact, if you continue doing what you've always done, you'll have what you've always had. That's just plain fact. If you want something different, then you'll have to turn around and do something different.

Start walking the road that says *God Straight Ahead*—not one where you sing que sera sera or what will be, will be. Decide it's turnaround time for you. From your head to your toes, from your pocketbook to your life-style, jerk yourself in line with God's Word. If you need a turnaround in your body, flood yourself with healing scriptures. If you need a turnaround in your marriage or relationships or finances, line your thinking up with God's Word in those areas. That's *how* you turn around. Quit thinking like you were before; that's what got you in trouble in the first place. Establish your heart in God, and put actions to your faith.

Psalm 1:3 says when you put God first, you'll be like "...a tree planted by the rivers of water, that brings forth its fruit in its season, whose leaf also shall not wither; and whatever he does shall prosper." This is the road for you.

ACTION ▷ ···

What three things will make a big turnaround in your life? Don't wait and think about it. Own up! And write it down now while the Holy Ghost is talking to you.

1._____

2._____

3._____

(34) | TURNAROUND TIME 2

So repent (change your mind and purpose); turn around and return [to God], that your sins may be erased (blotted out, wiped clean), that times of refreshing (of recovering from the effects of heat, of reviving with fresh air) may come from the presence of the Lord.
Acts 3:19 AMP

After Luke talked to us about turning around, he told us the next thing we need to do is leave our past behind. God is able to wipe our slates clean no matter what we've done. Actually, the born-again Christian doesn't even have a past with God, and it's important to recognize that. And if we stumble or fall, we sure don't need to stay down.

In fact, if you can ride a bicycle today, you learned because the first time you smacked the sidewalk you decided to try again. When you fell, you hopped back on that bike and tried again and again. That's a lesson a lot of Christians need to learn. When you're walking with God and you fall, God isn't sitting up in heaven with a big stick ready to whop you saying, "You messed up. You're out of the family!" No. First John 1:9 is every Christian's best friend and promises that when you ask for forgiveness, God is faithful and just to forgive you.

Nevertheless, the devil will try to beat you over the head with past mistakes until you feel so guilty you can't worship God. I've heard folks say, "I feel so unworthy." Well, don't! You don't have to *feel* worthy because God made you worthy. All you have to do is say, "Father, I'm so sorry. Forgive me," and turn around. No matter what's happened in your life, don't stay down for the count. *Get up!* Life deals some pretty hard blows now and then, and you may get knocked off your feet. But get back up and start walking with God and keep on walking with God into the happily ever after He has planned for you.

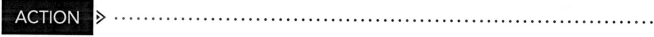 **ACTION** ▷ ·

To walk a new or better road with God, what are three things you need to leave behind?

(35) | TURNAROUND TIME 3

So repent (change your mind and purpose); turn around and return [to God], that your sins may be erased (blotted out, wiped clean), that times of refreshing (of recovering from the effects of heat, of reviving with fresh air) may come from the presence of the Lord.
Acts 3:19 AMP

Have you ever been stuck in a stuffy room feeling like you couldn't breathe when suddenly a window was opened and a cool breeze blew through? Or have you been outside on a hot, sultry day wishing you could jump into a pool of cool, blue water? The presence of the Lord is even better! It revives, refreshes and recovers you from the effects of heat. Peter tells us in Acts 3:19 that reviving is an important part of turning around and moving in a new direction.

The word *revive* means *to bring back to life or consciousness; to impart new health, vigor or spirit to; to return to effectiveness, or operative condition.* That's what Acts 3:19 says the presence of God does for us. Sometimes in life the heat is turned up full blast, and I'm not talking about the thermostat. I'm talking about the pressures of life and STRESS, in all capital letters. Yet that's not God's plan for His children. He did not create us to handle stress, but God has the solution for it just the same. The best stress reliever around is the presence of the Lord. He will help us recover from the heat and return us to effectiveness if we're lagging.

Keep in mind that getting in the presence of God takes time. The best things in life don't always come quickly, but they're so worth the time we invest. As we read earlier, Psalm 16:11 says, "...in thy presence is fulness of joy; at thy right hand there are pleasures for evermore" (KJV). One encounter with God will spin you around and send you going the right way in life.

If you're born again and Spirit filled, you are wall-to-wall God on the inside. Nevertheless, you can go from glory to glory enjoying the tangible anointing or manifested presence of God in your home, car, office and church. You were made to live in the presence of God. That's where you belong.

ACTION ▷ ···

Spend some time today in the presence of God. Read the Word, pray or worship to anointed music until you're quiet. Then be still and enjoy His presence. He will revive you.

We cannot spend time in the presence of God without coming away refreshed and enhanced. Write down what the Holy Ghost quickened to your heart today.

_____

_____

_____

_____

_____

(36) | FEAR TO FAITH

Do not be afraid; only believe.
Mark 5:36

Jesus spoke powerful words of faith to a father in Mark 5. As Jesus was ministering, a messenger came to tell the father, "Your daughter is dead. Why trouble the Teacher any further?" As soon as Jesus heard the word that was spoken, He said to [this father] … and ruler of the synagogue, "Do not be afraid; only believe" (Mark 5:35-36). In other words, Jesus told the father and us that fear paralyzes but faith liberates.

Let me tell you this story about how badly fear can paralyze. Although I didn't recognize it for a long time, I had a fear of big dogs all my life. Frankly, I would run the opposite direction if I saw one coming my way at the park or on a sidewalk. So, it's pretty ironic that I now have my second big—actually huge—dog. Our first dog, Dakota, was a 155-pound Great Pyrenees. Our second dog, Cherokee, is a 115-pound Newfoundland.

My sister, Renee, especially thinks it's funny that Mark and I have owned two big dogs since she remembers that I never even liked dogs. In fact, Renee reminded me one day just how much I used to dislike dogs. She said when we were little girls riding our bicycles around the neighborhood there was a German Shepherd who chased us. I don't remember any of this, but Renee, who is five years younger, said one bark from that dog and she would pedal home as fast as her legs would carry her. But she would look back to see me frozen in the middle of the road. "You would pedal to a certain point and then just stop like you were paralyzed," she said. I was paralyzed—with fear.

That's the trouble with fear. It leaves people paralyzed and unable to move and act, which is true in life way beyond bicycles and dogs. When some folks are given a bad report from the doctor or symptoms attack their bodies, fear grips them. It paralyzes them and leaves them frozen and unable to operate even in faith. But I'll tell you what. When faith comes, it liberates and overcomes fear every single time.

"How do I get unparalyzed?" someone asks. You get in faith! Romans 10:17 says faith comes by hearing and hearing the Word of God. Get out your Bible and look up what God says about whatever is trying to scare you. As you hear—and keep hearing—what God says, faith will come. It just happens. You can't stop it. If you're struggling to believe, you just haven't heard enough.

God has not given you the spirit of fear, but He did say, "For whatever is born of God overcomes the world. And this is the victory that has overcome the world—our faith" (1 John 5:4). You can always trust God. Not one word of His good promise has ever failed to come to pass (1 Kings 8:56).

ACTION ▷ ···

Take a minute to right down your fears and confront them with God's Word!

FEAR	TRUTH

(37) | CROSS OVER

On the same day, when evening had come, He said to them, "Let us cross over to the other side." Now when they had left the multitude, they took Him along in the boat as He was. And other little boats were also with Him. And a great windstorm arose, and the waves beat into the boat, so that it was already filling. But He was in the stern, asleep on a pillow. And they awoke Him and said to Him, "Teacher, do You not care that we are perishing?" Then He arose and rebuked the wind, and said to the sea, "Peace, be still!" And the wind ceased and there was a great calm. But He said to them, "Why are you so fearful? How is it that you have no faith?"

Mark 4:35-41

After Jesus woke up and calmed the storm, He gave his disciples a faith lesson that we all can use. Jesus asked them, *"Why are you so fearful? How is it that you have no faith?"* Actually, Jesus was making the point that fear and faith are opposites, and there's no room for both in the same boat. Fear will rob your faith.

Jesus had already told the disciples, "Guys, let's cross over." Jesus did not say, "Hey, let's see *if* we can make it." In other words, the disciples had God's Word on the subject just as you already have God's Word on whatever you're facing. The problem was the disciples got their eyes off God's Word and on the winds and waves. They got scared because of what they saw happening around them.

We've all done that. Actually, several years ago we were in a boat on an Oklahoma lake feeling a lot like the disciples. It had been a beautiful afternoon, when suddenly we saw dark clouds overhead, and I thought, *Oh my lands! We better outrun what looks to be a nasty storm!"* Unfortunately, we ran straight into the storm on the middle of the lake. It was not good.

Keep in mind that I grew up on the Gulf Coast and know all about huge waves, but the waters that day were *bad.* The calm lake we had enjoyed turned into billowing waves and swirling winds. Waves were dumping into our boat, and I was afraid. Another couple was with us, and the husband was calling out, "Jesus! Jesus! Jesus!"

while the wife prayed loudly. Mark was doing his best to steer the boat while I was calling out, "Get me off of this lake! Get me to the other side *now!* Never moved by anything, Mark stared straight ahead calmly and peacefully as always.

Lightning flashed! Thunder boomed! Then smack—we hit a sandbar. Suddenly we were stuck looking like something out of the old TV show *Gilligan's Island.* Before long another boat, also hightailing it home, turned around to help us. They stopped on another sandbar, waded toward us and pulled us out, thank God. We headed for home and lived to tell about it. But by the time we pulled into the dock, I was still so afraid my knees were shaking. I couldn't even put weight on my legs; I just sat there. The nightmare was all over, but fear had me absolutely paralyzed.

I understood the disciples in Mark 4 like never before. Sure, they had a Word from God. I had one, too. Psalm 91 promises me protection in everything all the time, but in the middle of the storm, I was faced with tremendous fear. The reality is that thoughts and fears come to us all. The point is, as Christians we already have God's Word, but do we act like it? Or do we allow fear to grip us and paralyze us?

The disciples would have understood my fear on the Oklahoma lake, and I understood theirs. Yet, frankly, we all have a choice. The storms of life come to all, and when they do, will we believe God's Word or what we see? Choose faith not fear. Faith is the boat that will help us cross over to victory every time.

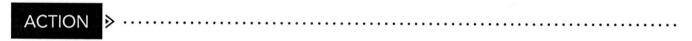

ACTION ▷

Spend some time confessing the scriptures you looked up yesterday. Confess them often. They will run off fear in your life!

(38) | WHAT DO YOU BELIEVE?

Who has believed our report?
And to whom has the arm of the Lord been revealed?
Isaiah 53:1

Life is all about choices. You already have God's guarantee for your health, prosperity, healing, safety and more. Yet, what report will you choose to believe when life challenges you? I shared about my *Gilligan's Island* adventure on the Oklahoma lake, and afterward I wrote myself this note about the disciples being afraid of the wind and the waves in Mark 4: "The disciples may not have had life preservers, but God's Word will be a life preserver to me."

God's Word did preserve the disciples, and they made it to the other side. In fact, we'll always make it to the other side *as long* as we believe God's Word. Really, the storm the disciples encountered didn't matter one way or another. It didn't matter that winds were blowing or waves were filling the boat. The storms in your life don't matter either. "How can you say that?" someone might ask. I can say it because Jesus told the disciples, "*We will cross* to the other side," and Jesus told you that *your faith is the victory* that overcomes the world.

Jesus has told you, "He Himself took our infirmities and bore our sicknesses" (Matthew 8:17). The Word says, "My God shall supply all your need according to His riches in glory" (Philippians 4:19). The Word says, "The Lord will perfect that which concerns me" (Psalm 138:8). The Word says, "If any of you lacks wisdom, let him ask of God, who gives to all liberally and without reproach, and it will be given to him" (James 1:5). The Word says, "If you can believe, all things *are* possible to him who believes" (Mark 9:23). All these scriptures were written for *you*, so what will *you* believe?

Isaiah 53:1 asks who will believe God's report? To that person who believes God, He will bare His arm and show His power. Mark often teaches that when a workman comes to your house, he rolls up his sleeves before he goes to work just as God bares His right arm of power to go to work in your circumstances. So make up your mind that you will cross over to victory in every situation. Make up your mind that you will live and not die.

Make up your mind that you will walk in health, prosperity and peace. If you will *only believe*, God will keep you from sinking every time.

ACTION ▷ ···

Is there an area where you need God to roll up His sleeves and go to work for you? Will you believe His report? What scripture(s) are you standing on?

_____

_____

_____

_____

_____

(39) | STOP, LOOK, LISTEN

But as it is written: "Eye has not seen, nor ear heard, Nor have entered into the heart of man The things which God has prepared for those who love Him." But God has revealed them to us through His Spirit. For the Spirit searches all things, yes, the deep things of God.
1 Corinthians 2:9-10

I've heard folks say, "I just can't seem to find the plan and purpose for my life." Yet, God says in our text He *has already* revealed His plans to us by the Holy Ghost in us. That means we *can* know—we already *do* know—God's will for our lives. Sometimes we just need to stop, look and listen to recognize it.

The Message says, "…We haven't stopped praying for you, asking God to give you *wise minds and spirits attuned to his will,* and so acquire a thorough understanding of the ways in which God works" (Colossians 1:9). I love that expression because it talks about us becoming attuned to God's will, and we certainly can fine-tune our spirits to know the will of God for our lives.

In his book *The Guide Inside,* Mark shares the example of fine-tuning an old-fashioned car radio as he explains how to find and follow God's will for your life. Car radios back in the day had knobs so a person could turn a little this way or that to zero in on a station and eliminate noisy static. In the same way, we can fine-tune our spirits to hear from the Holy Spirit by praying in the Spirit. It makes us more sensitive to the Holy Ghost and helps us make adjustments and tweak our direction as God prompts us.

"How often do I have to pray in tongues?" First of all, you don't *have* to pray in tongues, you *get* to pray in tongues. And you should pray in the Spirit as often as you can; pray in the car, in the shower, walking the dog or getting dressed. Just pray. First Corinthians 14:2 says when you pray in tongues, you're speaking divine secrets and mysteries to God. Maybe you don't understand, but God does. How awesome that we can speak to God straight from our hearts, which is how we bring the direction, plans and wisdom that God has imparted in our spirits, into this realm where we can walk it out.

ACTION ▷ ....

Share out of your heart below the direction you already know God has given you. It will do you good to pull the direction out of your heart and see it in black and white. It will also do you good down the road to look back and see how much more light was revealed to you as you continued to pray.

_____

_____

_____

_____

_____

(If you desire more teaching on following God's plan for your life or praying in the Spirit, consider *The Guide Inside* by Mark Brazee or *Tongues—Language of the Supernatural* by Janet Brazee.)

(40) | TRAFFIC LIGHTS

For as many as are led by the Spirit of God, these are sons of God.
Romans 8:14

If you're a born-again Christian, imagine your spirit as a traffic light receiving signals from the Spirit of God who makes His home in you. His direction is often just like a traffic light with green, yellow or red lights to alert you. If you'll follow these Holy Ghost signals, you'll be able to follow Him into God's best for your life.

A green light, so to speak, tells us to keep moving, all is well; it's a peaceful, velvety feeling in our spirits. A yellow light means caution, not so fast. Actually, to a lot of drivers a yellow light means hurry up before the light changes, but that shouldn't be the case when it comes to following our inward witness. When the signal is yellow, we need to slow down because there's a "scratch" or a hesitancy on the inside. Then there are times when we sense a red light on the inside, which clearly means to stop; there's no peace to proceed.

Actually, sometimes we have one signal that changes to another. For example, there are times in life when we begin moving in a certain direction and down on the inside it's like, *Yes, this is great. This is right.* But as we go further, we sense something is not right. What should we do? Stop! Go back to where it seemed right. Go back to where there was peace. If we're born again, we can trust our spirits to lead us because Paul said that we are filled with the knowledge of God's will (Colossians 1:9).

Where are you filled with this knowledge? In your spirit. Your spirit will know things even when your mind doesn't have a clue. So learn to have confidence in your spirit who is hearing from the Holy Ghost. He's your Guide inside, and you can trust Him. He knows more about your future than you know about your past.

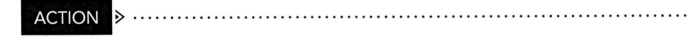

ACTION ⯈ ··

Stop! Check down inside. What is the Holy Ghost leading you to do? Are you being signaled with a green, yellow or red light?

(41) | BIG GOD

No matter what you're facing today, turn your attention to your BIG GOD. He's so much BIGGER than anything else competing for your attention. He's BIGGER than any problem. He's BIGGER than any question. He's BIGGER than any sickness. He's BIGGER than any financial need. He's not only the Greater One, but He's the Greater One *in you*.

Stop and praise Him now! Don't praise Him based on whether or not you feel like it. Praise Him because He's worthy, faithful and true. In fact, when it comes right down to it, you *need* to praise God. You see, God is doing just fine the way He is, but some situations in life hit us in the face and blur our vision. Challenges land on our paths to destroy us and sometimes they're so big they're all we can see. Sometimes they threaten to block our view of God. When that happens, there's no better time to magnify God.

Magnifying God changes our perception. It spins us around and gets us looking at the answer rather than the problem. That's when God is free to go to work in our circumstances and help us. That's when He can send angels to work in our lives, bringing the miraculous help we need.

Magnify God! Get your vision fixed! God is BIGGER than your problem. Whatever the problem, whatever the question, whatever the need, Jesus is the answer. He's your Healer. Waymaker. Leader. Provider. Redeemer. Deliverer. No matter what comes at you, He's still BIGGER. God is greater. Greater than what? Greater than whatever! And He said he would care for you (1 Peter 5:7) and cause you to triumph (2 Corinthians 2:14), so take Him at His Word.

ACTION ▷ ....

Meditate today on these three scriptures and let the Holy Ghost talk to you about them.

Isaiah 26:3 – "You will keep *him* in perfect peace, *Whose mind is stayed on You,* Because he trusts in You." The New Living Translation says, "You will keep in perfect peace all who trust in you, all *whose thoughts are fixed on you!*"

Numbers 21 – I encourage you to read this entire chapter in The Amplified Bible, focusing on verse 9, "And Moses made a serpent of bronze and put it on a pole, and if a serpent had bitten any man, when he looked to the serpent of bronze *[attentively, expectantly, with a steady and absorbing gaze]*, he lived." The Israelites received life for a look!

Proverbs 4:20-23 – "My son, pay attention to what I say; turn your ear to my words. *Do not let them out of your sight,* keep them within your heart; for they are life to those who find them and health to one's whole body. Above all else, guard your heart, for everything you do flows from it" (NIV).

What did the Holy Ghost speak to your heart?

_____

_____

_____

_____

_____

(42) | ENCOUNTERING FIRE

Call on the fire of God to ignite you. Call on the fire of God to change you. Call on the fire of God to stir you up and send you out. It worked for the early Church, and it will work for you. When fire came to sit on the 120 people in the Upper Room on the Day of Pentecost, they became saturated with God until they could sit no longer. They took to the streets and miracles began to flow.

Peter and John had the fire of God on them and took to the streets to see miracles. For many years a crippled man lay by the Gate Beautiful until one day they walked by him and said, "We're going to give you some of what we just got!" (Acts 3:6.) The man leaped up healed. Amazingly enough, that was the same Peter who denied Jesus three times a few days earlier. It was the same wimpy Peter who denied Jesus not to a band of soldiers but to a little girl. But Peter was wimpy no longer. He encountered the fire of God, and it changed him.

Moses also had an encounter with the fire of God, and it got him moving. Fire changed his entire calling. It thrust him from the backside of the desert into his God-ordained position as the deliverer of the children of Israel (Exodus 3). When Elijah had a showdown with the Prophets of Baal to establish whose God was real, the fire of God changed a whole nation in a day (1 Kings 18).

The fire of God will also change you and me. "But I'm so shy," someone might say. The fire of God will make us bold! The Spirit of the Lord will come upon us and change us into different people. It's not about us—it's all about Him. We're so blessed that it's important to not become selfish with what we have. We need to get off our blessed assurance and take what God has given us to the world.

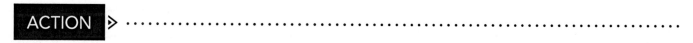

ACTION ▷ ···

It's time for you to take to the streets with the fire of God in you. Where will you go today? Ask the Holy Ghost for an assignment. Then such as you have, give!

(43) | RUNNING ON EMPTY

Ever felt like your spiritual tank is running low? Maybe you've lost your desire to read your Bible or go to church regularly. Maybe you've lost your desire to pray on a regular basis. Or maybe you just need your spiritual tank topped off. One thing is for sure. Whether we're talking about our spiritual tanks or gasoline tanks, running on fumes doesn't work. We need to fill up!

Let me tell you this little story. I'm actually the world's worst at paying attention to my car's gas gauge. In fact, a while back Mark and I were on our way to Claremore, Oklahoma, about 45 minutes outside of Tulsa. As we drove out of our neighborhood, Mark looked at the gas gauge and said, "We're getting low on gas, but we've got plenty to get to Claremore. We'll fill the tank before we head home."

As we got near Claremore, I dropped Mark off at a little coffee shop while I ran another errand. When I finished my errand, I called my sister to chat while on the way to pick up Mark. Unfortunately, before I knew it, I had driven through Claremore and taken the turnpike toward Tulsa without Mark. It's sad but true. Oh, yeah. I forgot my husband who was still back at the coffee shop.

There I was talking away to my sister—yada yada yada yada—right through the toll booth and—yada yada yada yada—right onto the highway. All of the sudden it dawned on me, *Oh, no! I forgot Mark!* The problem was that there was nowhere to turn around on the turnpike, and it was a long way to an exit. I didn't know what to do, so I called Mark and said, "Hey! You'll never believe what just happened."

"Did you get stopped by a train?" he asked, since I had been stopped by two recently.

"Well...not exactly," I said, feeling kind of sheepish.

"What then?" he asked.

"I'm on the turnpike."

"The turnpike?! Going which way?"

"West."

"Ok, well, just get off at the next exit and come back."

"Wait! There's a sign! Maybe it's an exit coming up! Oh, no, it says 'Grand Lake 15 miles.' Oh, well...."

About the same time it dawned on me, Mark said, "Wait! You're going east. You're going the wrong direction!" At that moment I wasn't really sure whether I was going east or west, but I was headed toward Joplin, Missouri, which is definitely the opposite direction of Tulsa.

"Just go until you get to the next exit," Mark said. "There's nothing else to do."

"But, Mark!" I said. "I'm low on gas. How long do I have when the light is on?"

"I don't know," he said, "We've never driven it that low before. I'm guessing 20-25 miles."

The whole story was like something out of an *I Love Lucy* episode, but I finally made it back to town and picked up Mark. Together we headed for the nearest gas station.

The point is, God does not want us running our spiritual tanks on "E" either. He doesn't want us running out of spiritual fuel because He doesn't want us to face life alone. God wants our spiritual tanks full and topped off so we can benefit the most from the Holy Ghost as teacher, leader, guide and protector.

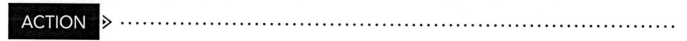

ACTION ▷

Time to check your spiritual tank. Are you running on empty, or are you full?

(44) | WHEN GOD COMES

I'm thanking you, GOD, from a full heart, I'm writing the book on your wonders.
I'm whistling, laughing, and jumping for joy; I'm singing your song, High God. The day my
enemies turned tail and ran, they stumbled on you and fell on their faces. You took over and
set everything right; when I needed you, you were there, taking charge.
Psalm 9:1-4 The Message

You don't have to be a Christian long to know that the devil is out to harass and hinder you whenever he can. First Peter 5:8 says he's like a roaring lion seeking whom he may devour. He doesn't show up in a red jumpsuit with a pitchfork. If he did, we would all know what to do. That would be easy. No, the devil comes at you with symptoms, thoughts, circumstances and situations; that's his entire arsenal.

I've noticed the devil especially likes to pester people in the middle of the night in the form of thoughts and fears, saying things like, "That pain is probably a terminal disease. Face it. You're dying. You're going to lose your job. You will go bankrupt and lose all you have. You'll never amount to anything. Your spouse wants to leave you. Your children will never serve God." The devil looks for someone to believe those lies, so don't let that someone be you.

Here's the good news. When we praise and worship, God comes. When God comes, trouble goes. In fact, the enemy is stopped in his tracks as we praise and worship. He has to get quiet and back off.

"What does praise and worship have to do with stopping the devil and shutting him up?" someone asks. Everything. When you praise God, negative thoughts have to go. They vanish into thin air because that's exactly what they are—a puff of smoke.

Recently, someone in our World Outreach Church congregation received a bad report from the doctor and asked me to agree in prayer for healing. "You've got it!" I said. But in my spirit I heard, *It's a smoke screen.* It was very faint, yet it was there. Every time I would get ready to pray about the situation, those words kept coming to me.

"What do you mean by a smoke screen?" It's a cloud of smoke that tries to cover up what's really going on. In this case, a smoke screen was trying to cover the truth of God's Word that says by Jesus' stripes we were healed (Isaiah 53:4-5, 1 Peter 2:24, Matthew 8:17). The person went back for a follow-up appointment, and doctors found absolutely nothing wrong. The devil is such a liar.

Try this with me. When I say *start*, begin slowly counting to 10 out loud. Start! Now say *praise the Lord!* out loud. What happened? Could you continue counting while you said *praise the Lord?* No. Your brain stopped to listen to the words coming out your mouth. So the next time the devil bombards your mind with thoughts—morning, noon or night—open your mouth and praise God right out loud. You'll zip the devil's lip. He will hightail it and run.

ACTION ▷ ··

Our text scripture above said, "I'm whistling, laughing, and jumping for joy; I'm singing your song, High God." How about it? Whistle! Laugh! Jump! Sing! God will come on the scene and "set everything right"!

45 | THROUGH AND THROUGH

I find that I'm safe and warm in Your loving arms.
You see me and You know me.
And You love me through and through. *

A young woman on our praise and worship team at World Outreach Church spontaneously sang the song above in a service one night, and the words really touched my heart. The message is simple but profound. God sees you. He knows you. He loves you.

Even when you feel all alone, God sees you exactly where you are. He promised He would never leave you or forsake you, and His ear is ever open to your cry. He never tells you to make an appointment or tells you, "Come back later. I'm too busy. I don't have time for you." God is available 24/7; He doesn't even sleep. In fact, no matter what you're facing, He's right in the middle of the situation with you, ready to lead you out to victory. He sees *you*.

God also knows you. No one knows you better, and no one else knows the plans He has to bless you and prosper you. Jeremiah 29:11 says, "For I know the plans I have for you," says the LORD. "They are plans for good and not for disaster, to give you a future and a hope" (NLT).

Most of all, God also loves you through and through. No one knows you better, and no one loves you more. When you love somebody, you'll go out of your way for them. God went out of His way for us when He sent Jesus to die for us so that we might live eternally. Before you were even born again, God loved you so much that He gave up His only Son for you. He knew that in doing so He would reap many sons and daughters.

Don't ever wonder again, *Does God really love me and care what I'm going through?* He sees you. He knows you. He loves you through and through. He knows the questions and struggles you have. He knows the fears that try to grip you. He knows it all, but nothing can stand in comparison to His love for you that knows no limits or end. His love for you never fails. He never gives up on you.

Think about it. He sees us, but He still doesn't give up on us. He knows us, but He still doesn't give up on us. He loves us, but He still doesn't give up on us. Spend time with Him, and He'll make you feel warm and safe.

ACTION ▷ ·

Put a little tune to these words and sing them throughout the day: *You see me. You know me. You love me through and through.*

*Words and music of *Through and Through* by Will Reagan of United Pursuit.

46 | EVERY PRAISE

Every praise is to our God.
Every word of worship with one accord,
Every praise, every praise is to our God.
Sing hallelujah to our God.
Glory hallelujah is due our God.
Every praise, every praise is to our God.
God my Savior,
God my Healer,
God my Deliverer,
Yes He is! Yes He is!*

A lot of people wake up in the morning thinking, *Oh, boy. Time to get up. Time to go to work. I dread work. Sigh. I hope today is better than yesterday.* So let me ask. How's that working for you? Instead, what if we woke up saying, "Hallelujah! Today will be a great day because the greater One lives in me (1 John 4:4). As He is so am I in this world (1 John 4:17). I win in every situation. You're my Savior! You're my healer! You're my Deliverer! Yes, you are! Every praise to You, my God."

I remember the story Mark tells of when he first got born again in college. He went back to his dorm and told his friends, "I got saved tonight."

"Saved from what?"

"I don't know. All I know is I got saved."

If you are a born-again Christian, you are saved from the hand of the enemy. You've been saved from hell. You've been pulled out of the kingdom of darkness and translated into the kingdom of light. The Spirit of God has come to live inside you, and you've been given the life, nature and ability of God on the inside. He is your

Savior. He is your Healer. He is your Deliverer. There's nothing too hard for Him, and every praise belongs to Him.

ACTION ▷ ···

List five specific things you can praise God for and then do it!

1._____

2._____

3._____

4._____

5._____

*Words and music for *Every Praise* by Hezekiah Walker.

(47) | GOODNESS

*Taste and see that the L*ORD *is* GOOD.
Oh, the joys of those who take refuge in him!
Psalm 34:8 NLT

I'm so thankful for the goodness of God. No matter what the situation, we can see His goodness. When God shows up on the scene, things change because goodness always changes things. So focus on what God has promised you and be confident that you will see God's goodness in your circumstances.

Your confidence in God's goodness will be like an anchor that sinks down deep and takes hold. When situations and symptoms come at you like the waves of the sea, don't feel like you will lose ground, float away or even drown; the goodness of God will hold you steady.

People may let you down in this life, but God will never let you down. People may not mean to hurt you, but they are human and sometimes they fail. Sometimes even family and the closest friends hurt us deeply, but you can always have confidence in God Almighty. God is good. True. Faithful and everlasting. He's never moody. He doesn't wake up on the wrong side of the bed. God is a good God *all the time!*

If you need answers today, ask Him for wisdom. If you are lonely and need friends, ask Him for divine connections. If you need healing, thank Him for the redemptive benefits Jesus provided on the cross. If you need financial help, thank Him for His provision. Open your mouth and open the door to the goodness of God.

ACTION ⟩ ....

God is all about goodness, and you should be, too. So as God brings goodness to you, then you should deliver goodness to another. Ask the Holy Ghost to show you where you can do good today.

(48) | SHOUT IT OUT

Oh, clap your hands, all you peoples!
Shout to God with the voice of triumph!
Psalm 47:1

Over and over in God's Word we are told to shout unto God with a voice of triumph, so have you ever wondered what the big deal is about shouting? The truth is, the shout can be a very supernatural thing.

I remember several years ago Mark and I attended a college football game with two young men from our church playing on the team. Never before had I heard such a roar of people shouting. When the team scored, you could probably hear the shouting miles away. I remember looking at Mark saying, "If we could only get people to praise God like this in church."

The crowd loved the game and the competition; we did, too. Yet, as good as the game was, all the cheering was over a little brown ball. As I listened that day to how the people in the stands loved rooting for their side, I began thinking how Christians also have a side. We are on God's side, and we're in a race to the finish. We even have a great cloud of witnesses cheering us on from the banisters of heaven.

Something else caught my attention during the football game. I never heard the opposing team shout when our team scored. You also don't hear defeated teams shout. Even more to the point, defeated Christians don't shout either. That's because the shout is an outward sign of victory. That's why you need to open your mouth and shout with a voice of triumph.

In Joshua 6 God told the Israelites to walk around the wall of Jericho and not say a word. Then on the seventh time around, God told them to shout. When they circled around the seventh time, those walls were still standing; nothing had changed. But as they shouted the walls tumbled down because there's power in the shout. So whatever situation you're facing, shout with a voice of triumph. Mountains will move, and things will change. You have God's Word on it.

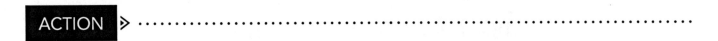

ACTION

Get up out of your chair and shout to the Lord with a voice of triumph. Act like you would if the answer was on its way because it is!

(49) | SUPERNATURAL INSURANCE

Psalm 91 is the best insurance policy around. If you mix your faith with Psalm 91 you'll have one supernatural insurance policy that works 365/24/7 with angels to back it up.

I doubt anyone would argue the need for an insurance policy in this day and time. It's no time to coast along spiritually. We're living in challenging days and perilous times, which is why we need to declare, "...I know whom I have believed and am persuaded He is able to keep what I have committed to Him..." (2 Timothy 1:12).

In fact, if you're someone who has spent years thinking, *I don't really know what I believe,* you better find out. We're living in the last of the last days, and you need your feet planted on solid ground. You need to make sure your life is built on the solid rock of Jesus Christ.

Raised on the Gulf Coast, I know a little something about solid foundations, and I've lived through many hurricanes. Most houses on the beach were built on stilts, so after most hurricanes, they were no more. Why? Those houses were built on sand and didn't have a sure foundation. There is only one sure foundation that will stand the test of time: JESUS.

Don't let television news or newspaper headlines convince you otherwise. Don't let fear enter your heart because of bad news. Build your faith on God, the everlasting Father, because with Him you can weather any storm or calamity life brings along. This is no day to simply cruise along playing church. It's a day and an hour when you must know what you believe, and you must refuse to let anything – including fear – move you off of it.

John G. Lake, 20th century apostle to Africa, lived in a day when the bubonic plague raged in Africa, and people were dying left and right by the thousands. Yet, Rev. Lake knew the life of God was inside him. He knew the same Spirit that raised Jesus from the dead lived in him. In fact, he was so bold that in order to demonstrate the healing power of God, he had germs placed in his hand and said, "Let me show you what the life of God can do." As he held the foamy plague for all to see, every germ died while doctors and scientists looked on. The life of God in him caused those cells to die instantly.

You and I need to build our faith in this very same life of God and live *The God Life*. Don't wait until trouble comes to find out what you believe. Develop strong faith now in God's supernatural insurance policy before trouble ever knocks at your door.

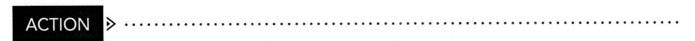

ACTION ▷ ....

Read and mediate on Psalm 91 today. I enjoy reading the The Message translation below. Find the version you like best and commit it to memory. Hide it in your heart. Psalm 91 will keep you safe.

You who sit down in the High God's presence, spend the night in Shaddai's shadow, Say this: "God, you're my refuge. I trust in you and I'm safe!" That's right—he rescues you from hidden traps, shields you from deadly hazards. His huge outstretched arms protect you—under them you're perfectly safe; his arms fend off all harm. Fear nothing—not wild wolves in the night, not flying arrows in the day, Not disease that prowls through the darkness, not disaster that erupts at high noon. Even though others succumb all around, drop like flies right and left, no harm will even graze you. You'll stand untouched, watch it all from a distance, watch the wicked turn into corpses. Yes, because God's your refuge, the High God your very own home, Evil can't get close to you, harm can't get through the door. He ordered his angels to guard you wherever you go. If you stumble, they'll catch you; their job is to keep you from falling. You'll walk unharmed among lions and snakes, and kick young lions and serpents from the path. "If you'll hold on to me for dear life," says God, "I'll get you out of any trouble. I'll give you the best of care if you'll only get to know and trust me. Call me and I'll answer, be at your side in bad times; I'll rescue you, then throw you a party. I'll give you a long life, give you a long drink of salvation!"

⑤⓪ | THE FIXER

The LORD will perfect that which concerns me....
Psalm 138:8

By nature I'm a fixer. If I see someone going through a hard time, I want to help fix it. Unfortunately, most people's situations are bigger and more involved than a human can fix. Yet, there's always one solution that works: "Father, I put my trust in You."

If you can trust God with where you will spend eternity, then you can trust Him with everything else in life. The whole reason Jesus came to this earth was to provide you with abundant life. It's the devil who tries to steal, kill and destroy you.

"But I don't know how God could fix this mess!" someone might say. That's why our Christian walk is a walk of faith. Of course we cannot figure it all out, but we know who can. Speaking of God figuring things out, Isaiah 40:12 says, "Who has measured the waters in the hollow of His hand, measured heaven with a span and calculated the dust of the earth in a measure? Weighed the mountains in scales and the hills in a balance?" I think calculating the earth and arranging the galaxies more than qualifies God to handle whatever problems threaten our peace of mind.

Folks, God is the supreme Fixer of all time. He's more than able to handle situations and circumstances that confront us. All we have to do is get out of His way, turn our situation over to Him in faith and thank Him the answer is on the way.

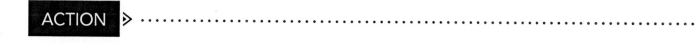

ACTION ▷ ....

Jot down the day and time you released your faith and turned over your situation to the Fixer of all time. Then be sure to come back and jot down your testimony of how amazingly well God went to work in your behalf. Above all, don't keep a good testimony to yourself. Be sure to share it with others!

(51) | BROKEN HEARTS

There's a little chorus that simply says: *There is none like You. No one else can touch my heart like You do. I could search for all eternity long and find there is none like You.** I love those words, but my most favorite line is, "No one else can touch my heart like you do."

Only God really knows our hearts. He knows our real intents and motives. He knows our plans and purposes. He knows our deepest loves and feelings, and He's the One who deals with us heart to heart. He also knows when we have a broken heart—when something has hurt us and wounded us.

Broken hearts are very real, and don't ever let anyone tell you different. The good news is that broken hearts don't have to stay broken. If your heart is broken, the Spirit of God can heal it. In fact, there's no one else who can heal a broken heart like Him. There's no spouse, friend, child, minister or counselor who can help you the way He can because some things in this life don't come by might or power, but by His Spirit touching us at our very core.

ACTION ▷ ....

If you need your heart healed today, pray with me now: *Dear Father, I come to You today with a broken heart, and I ask for Your help. As an act of my will, I choose right now in Jesus' name to forgive, forget and let go of the situation or individual who wounded my heart. Now, I ask the Holy Ghost to come and do what only He can do. Thank You.*

Begin to worship! Bask in His presence. Never can we encounter His presence and come away unchanged.

*Words and music for *There is None Like You* by Lenny LeBlanc.

⑤② | HUGS

Hugs are a good thing, and I should know because I'm a hugger from way back. There are just times and situations in life when hugs are required. Life can get crazy busy as we get wrapped up in a world of details, but a hug is just the pause we need.

I can't tell you how many times I've been almost flying through the house getting ready to race out the door, and Mark will stop me in my tracks.

"What? What? What? I'm in a hurry," I say.

"Just stop!" he says, walking over to me. He puts his arms around me and locks them tightly.

I usually try to wrestle away saying, "I don't have time for this!" But he doesn't let go and holds me in a bear hug until I stop squirming.

"Ok, I'm stopped!" I say finally.

"Take three breaths," he says.

I used to say, "You've got to be kidding me?" But I don't say that anymore because he's done this so many times I know what's coming. I'm telling you what, by the third breath, a peace starts to come over me. I slow down and know all is well.

In the same way, we can run into the arms of our Father God. Actually, unfortunately, there are times we try to wrestle away from the Father's arms. Instead, we should learn to run to Him and stay a while because His arms are a good place to be. God has us covered, and we need to be still and quiet there, knowing all is well.

ACTION ▷ ···

Run to your heavenly Father and let Him love you. He loves and cares for you like no other. It also wouldn't hurt to ask for a hug from someone near and dear.

(53) | SAY SO

Let the redeemed of the Lord say so....
Psalm 107:2

In the 1970s there was a move of God that brought a strong emphasis on teaching and faith to the body of Christ, and I learned so much during that time about the power of our words. We learned that we can have what we say in this life, and we learned we will never rise above our confession. I devoured books on faith and our words. It turned my life around and did the same for many others.

Yet, as time passed, so many of those same people became "have hearders." In other words, too many people heard the Word of God, but did not continue it. We could say it went in one ear and out the other. But, folks, that won't do at all! Romans 10:17 says "faith comes by hearing, and hearing by the Word of God." Think about this. If faith comes by hearing, how does it go? It goes by not hearing.

These days when the principles of faith are shared, many folks slip over into a mentality of "Yeah, yeah, yeah, I've heard that before." But the whole point is that we cannot leave behind the basics that made us who we are and brought us where we are. Believing and saying are not basics that we outgrow; they are how we got born again and how we walk by faith. Faith is not an elementary principle that we leave behind. God says the just *shall live* by faith; it's to be our lifestyle.

The apostle Paul said, "We having the same spirit of faith, according as it is written, I believed, and therefore have I spoken; we also believe, and therefore speak" (2 Corinthians 4:13 KJV).

ACTION ▷ ···

Meditate on these faith-filled passages: James 3, Matthew 12, Mark 11, Matthew 21. Then rise up and declare some things today for your nation, your church, your family and your life.

(54) | REDEMPTION CENTER

…God sent forth His Son, born of a woman, born under the law, to redeem those who were under the law, that we might receive the adoption as sons. And because you are sons, God has sent forth the Spirit of His Son into your hearts, crying out, "Abba, Father!" Therefore you are no longer a slave but a son, and if a son, then an heir of God through Christ.
Galatians 4:4-7

Mark tells the story of going to an S&H Green Stamp redemption center when he was a kid to redeem green stamps for prizes. Back then grocery stores and other local businesses gave customers green stamps with purchases to encourage business. The idea was to collect the stamps in books and eventually exchange them to buy items from a catalog. Ultimately, the redemption center is where folks received the catalog items money couldn't buy.

Mark's mom, Ginny, collected whole grocery bags full of green stamps that she gave him to put into books because he really wanted a sleeping bag he had seen in one of the catalogs. Mark still remembers licking and licking stamps to fill 20 some books to take to the redemption center. A person could go to the redemption center with all the gold in Fort Knox, but no deal would be made. They didn't want gold, silver or money. Green stamps were the only price that could be paid.

In the same way, when Adam sinned and mankind was separated from God, only one price could redeem us. God could have offered all the gold, silver or cattle on a thousand hills, but nothing but the precious blood of Jesus could redeem us. Humanity was locked away in a redemption center, and nobody on Earth could redeem us. But God so loved the world that He sent His only son Jesus to redeem us (John 3:16).

Isaiah 53:4-5 says, "Surely He has borne our griefs and carried our sorrows; yet we esteemed Him stricken, smitten by God, and afflicted. But He was wounded for our transgressions, He was bruised for our iniquities; the chastisement for our peace was upon Him, and by His stripes we are healed." Jesus redeemed us from anything that would destroy our peace of mind, and He was made poor so that through His poverty we might be abundantly supplied.

This means that sin has no right in your life. Sickness has no right to come on you. Poverty has no right to rob you. Depression has no right to harass you. When these things try to sneak into your life, open your mouth and say, "Christ has redeemed me from the curse of the law!" (Galatians 3:13).

ACTION ▷ ···

Read the curse of the law in Deuteronomy 28 so you can appreciate just how free you really are. Then read Isaiah 53:4-5 and consider looking it up in different translations to really understand it. Write it out below in your favorite translation. Get a hold of it. Memorize it. Keep it in your heart and in your mouth.

_____

_____

_____

_____

_____

(55) | HEALING IS A FACT

Christ has redeemed us from the curse of the law....
Galatians 3:13

Jesus Christ has redeemed us from every one of the awful curses listed in Deuteronomy 28 that includes every disease and plague known to mankind as well as future ones yet to come. Yet, before Jesus paid the price for our healing on the cross, the Old Testament promised the Israelites that *God will, God can, God should, God would* heal. But the New Testament says *Jesus did.* Healing is no longer a promise but a fact. Jesus *already provided*—past tense—healing. Now it's only ours to receive.

Before you were a Christian you might have said, "I sure hope God will heal me. I sure hope God can pull me out of this depression. But if you're born again, then you should be saying, "I am the redeemed of the Lord. Jesus provided forgiveness for my sins, healing for my body and peace for my mind all in one big package deal. He's already done it! It's mine, and I take it now by faith!"

"You're absolutely right!" someone might say. "I know God promised to heal me." No, He didn't. God *did not promise* to heal you; He just went ahead and did it. "Christ *has redeemed* us from the curse of the law, having become a curse for us (for it is written, 'Cursed *is* everyone who hangs on a tree'), that the blessing of Abraham might come upon the Gentiles in Christ Jesus, that we might receive the promise of the Spirit through faith" (Galatians 3:13-14). Healing is a done deal. It belongs to you. Reach out by faith and receive.

ACTION ▷ ....

Meditate on these scriptures that will be health and healing to you. One verse or phrase may stand out and be quickened to you. Hold on to it. Speak it over and over until it drops from your head to your heart, and then let your faith to do the talking!

Proverbs 4:20-24 | Matthew 8 | Galatians 3:13-14 | 1 Peter 2:24 | Psalm 107:20 | Romans 8:11

56 | HA HA HA HA HA

I love to laugh, and I do a lot of it. You should, too. It's good for us. Proverbs 17:22 says a cheerful heart is good medicine, and we should take our medicine more often. We should have glad written all over us because we've got a lot to be glad about. God Himself is glad and "…breaks out laughing" as His enemies are scattered and confused (Psalm 2:4 The Message).

Psalm 126:1-3 says, "When the Lord brought back the captivity of Zion, we were like those who dream. Then our mouth was filled with laughter, and our tongue with singing. Then they said among the nations, 'The Lord has done great things for them.' The Lord has done great things for us, and we are glad." That's right! The Lord has done great things for them—*and us*. Our captivity was turned 2,000 years ago when Jesus rose from the dead. "But I'm waiting to be delivered!" Wait no longer. Jesus set us free! The only thing left to do is fill our mouths with laughter and our tongues with singing.

Psalm 35:27 says, "Let them shout for joy and be glad, who favor my righteous cause; and let them say continually, 'Let the Lord be magnified, who has pleasure in the prosperity of His servant.'" If you feel like a nasty cloud has been hanging over your head, begin "giving thanks unto the Father, which hath made us meet to be partakers of the inheritance of the saints in light: Who hath [*already, already, already*] delivered us from the power of darkness, and hath [*already*] translated us into the kingdom of his dear Son" (Colossians 1:12-13 KJV).

ACTION ▷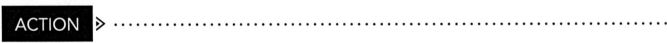

Laugh! You need to laugh! Need help getting started? Find something funny to watch or read or visit friends who make you laugh. Just get off your blessed assurance and get glad! It will be medicine for you.

(57) | NO TRESPASSING

There are times when it seems like sickness and disease run rampant. There are especially times of the year when it seems that people all over the country are coming down with something. It attacks their sinuses. It attacks their throats and voices. It attacks their whole bodies. But sickness and disease should have no part of us. The devil is trespassing on God's property. He crosses over the line when he tries to put nasty symptoms on us. Sickness doesn't belong to us. We've been redeemed by the blood of Jesus.

I've heard folks talk about getting shots to head off different ailments, and that's fine. There's nothing wrong with that, but at the same time, as believers we also need to ward off sickness by being full of faith and full of the Holy Ghost. We need to wake up every morning saying, "I am the healed of the Lord. I am healed from the top of my head to the soles of my feet. I am redeemed by the precious blood of Jesus. Himself took my infirmities and bear my sicknesses. He sent His Word and healed me. The devil can't trespass on this property because I belong to God."

Acts 10:38 says, "How God anointed Jesus of Nazareth with the Holy Spirit and with power, who went about doing good and healing all who were oppressed by the devil, for God was with Him." The good news is that Jesus is still healing today. He's still setting free the oppressed today. He's got good news for you today because "Jesus Christ is the same yesterday, today, and forever" (Hebrews 13:8).

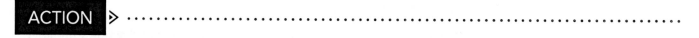

ACTION ▷ ....

Declare with your mouth, "No, you don't, devil! You're not trespassing on this property. I'm drawing the line, and you're on the other side in Jesus' name." Don't you forget—and don't let the devil forget—that you're not *trying* to get healed; you have *already been* healed. Just receive what's already been provided for you and act like the Word is true!

(58) | HE KEEPS ME SINGING

A while back I came across an article telling the story of L.B. Bridgers who wrote the classic song *He Keeps Me Singing*.* I was so blessed by it and want to share an abbreviated version of the story with you.

"I learned that Gospel songs that touch the heart are not always written simply out of sheer delight and happiness, but often come from devastating tragedy, great disappointment or anguish in the writer's life. So it was quite a shock to me when I learned the story behind the upbeat hymn, *He Keeps Me Singing*. My thought was that the writer simply sat down at his kitchen table some bright sunny morning, and with a cup of coffee next to him and rays of sunlight filling the room, he began to write cheerful words of this hymn.

"I was wrong! Behind this song – and as you may find to be true for many other Gospel songs – you'll find no happy circumstances. Yet, you'll discover the writer's joy of the Lord. L. B. (Luther Burgess) Bridgers, writer of this song, was born in 1884. Young Luther soon went into the ministry, attended Asbury College and met his wife. Over the next few years, this young married couple had three sons.

"During one particular call to minister, his wife and three sons traveled with him as far as Kentucky while he continued on. Near the end of that two-week revival, 27-year-old Bridgers received a telegram stating for him to 'COME HOME' to Middlesboro where his family was staying. After he made that quick trip, others meeting him at the train station gave him the bad news of a raging fire that claimed the lives of his wife and their three sons. All that remained of that house were the outer steps.

"As he visited the site, naturally Bridgers requested to be alone. Seated there a good while amidst the smoldering ashes and the devastating surroundings, Bridgers eventually removed from his suit pocket the very last letter he had received from his precious wife. Then after a time, Bridgers reached into another pocket and retrieved a pencil. He then turned the envelope over to write words on the blank side; words of what would later become part of a treasured hymn of the Church. This heartbroken man slowly wrote – 'There's within my heart a melody, JESUS whispers sweet and low, Fear not, I am with thee, peace be still, In all of life's ebb and flow.'

"By beginning to write words of that song that day, was Bridgers' mind free from thoughts on all he had lost just hours before? Of course not! He had lost his entire immediate family, so it was expected he would be troubled. But he did NOT give up or lose hope in God.

"This horrific disaster caused Bridgers to face unbelievable heartache, but through it all God gave him words of this song that have been shared throughout the ages. Whatever it may be that you and your family are facing today, may you ever keep in mind the wonderful name spoken in the chorus of Bridgers' song: 'JESUS, JESUS, JESUS, sweetest name I know, Fills my ev'ry longing, Keeps me singing as I go.' Thanking God for the Sweetest Name I know — JESUS!"

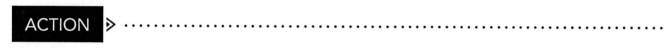

ACTION ⟩

If you know the song, sing it. If you don't, google the classic hymn.

Thank God for the sweetest name you know. No matter the circumstances in life, He's always kept me singing, and He'll do the same for you.

* The original article, *The Church Hymnal: He Keeps Me Singing,* was written by Bill Lloyd and published in *Absolutely Gospel Music* in 2013. This version is abridged.

(59) | OVERCOME OR OVERCOMER

For whatever is born of God overcomes the world.
And this is the victory that has overcome the world—our faith.
1 John 5:4

The Word of God says we've been made to be overcomers. It does not say we are in the process of overcoming or that we will someday overcome. No. It says that we *are* overcomers (Romans 8:37).

Sometimes we get overwhelmed, and we feel totally overcome. And yet, who made us to be overcomers? JESUS. He came to this earth and overcame for us. "For this purpose the Son of God was manifested, that He might destroy the works of the devil" (1 John 3:8). Then Jesus turned power and authority over to us (Luke 9:1-2). Then He raised us to sit in heavenly places with Him where the devil is under our feet (Ephesians 1:22; 2:6).

Therefore, we walk in victory in every situation. As long as you live in this earth, problems and challenges will come. But when those problems and challenges rise up, don't lay down so they roll over you. Rise up and use your authority. Cast down imaginations and anything that exalts itself against the name of Jesus (2 Corinthians 10:4-5).

If we just sit back and say, "what will be, will be," then we *will be* overcome. But Jesus has given you authority. He gave you His name, and He expects you to use it.

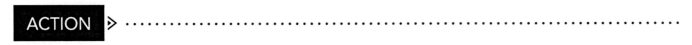

ACTION ≫ ··

Study these scriptures that talk about the overcomer you are and then describe in your own words how God sees you.

Romans 8:37 – "But in all these things we **overwhelmingly conquer** through Him who loved us" (NASB).

1 John 4:4 – "You are from God, little children, and have **overcome them,** because He who is in you is greater than he who is in the world."

Revelation 12:11 – "They **overcame him** by the blood of the Lamb and by the word of their testimony, and they did not love their lives to the death."

_____

_____

_____

_____

_____

(60) | PARADOX

God wants you and I to confound this world's way of thinking and demonstrate His way of thinking. Actually, God has planned that we be a walking and talking paradox on this earth. The word *paradox*, according to The American Heritage Dictionary, means *a statement that seems to contradict itself that is nonetheless true.* That's exactly what we become in our Christian walk.

After all, *to really live, we must die* because Galatians 2:20 says, "I have been crucified with Christ; it is no longer I who live, but Christ lives in me…."

To be wise, we must become fools because 1 Corinthians 3:18 says, "…If anyone among you seems to be wise in this age, let him become a fool that he may become wise."

To be exalted, we must become humble for Matthew 23:12 says, "…whoever exalts himself will be humbled, and he who humbles himself will be exalted.

To be first, we must be last, for Matthew 20:16 says, "So the last will be first, and the first last. For many are called, but few chosen."

To get, we must give because Luke 6:38 says, "Give, and it will be given to you: good measure, pressed down, shaken together, and running over will be put into your bosom. For with the same measure that you use, it will be measured back to you."

The truth is, when our *natural* abilities end, we can become the *supernatural* contradiction to this world that God intends for us to be.

ACTION ▷ ....

In the left column below, write down ways you or others might describe you naturally. In the right column, write down how God describes you supernaturally.

NATURAL YOU	SUPERNATURAL — PARADOX — YOU

⑥⑦ | IT'S YOUR TIME

...You have come to the kingdom for such a time as this....
Esther 4:14

It's no accident that you are alive today. It's no accident you were born in this generation and not in the 1700s or 1800s. There's a divine purpose and a divine destiny on your life, and you've come to the kingdom for such a time as this.

A young Jewish girl named Esther heard similar words. She had been selected from among many girls to meet the king who was looking for a queen. Esther was chosen, and it was a good thing for the entire Jewish nation. One of the king's advisers had devised a plan to kill the Jews, but God gave Esther great favor. She had the ears of the king. As a result, she saved the Jews from destruction.

The interesting thing is that Esther becoming queen was the small picture, which is all we see sometimes from our human point of view. The bigger picture—God's picture—was that Esther was positioned as queen by God to fulfill a divine purpose.

We need to take a lesson from Esther. We need to quit looking at the small picture and look at the big picture. So often God directs us to a city or a nation as part of His divine plan, but we're tempted to complain about the weather, the city, the job and all the mundane details. Yet, none of those details really matter because God is working out the bigger picture. God is working out His divine plan and purpose for our lives.

It's time to take the limits off. Think BIG. Think like God thinks. Be confident in the fact that God knows more about your future than you know about your past. Trust Him. If you've followed God to the place where you are, then you're positioned for a purpose. Make sure you recognize His divine destiny on you. He has big plans for you, and He'll lead you one step at a time.

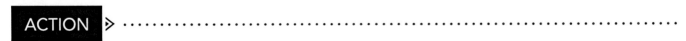

ACTION ⟩ ....

In what areas of your life should you take the limits off? Write them down and watch God go to work.

_____

_____

_____

_____

_____

⬤62 | GO FISH!

...I will make you fishers of men.
Matthew 4:19

Jesus told two brothers one day, "I will make you fishers of men." His offer still holds. Jesus will teach you to fish for souls if you will let Him. I want Him to teach me. How about you?

Actually, I love to fish. I bait my own hook and cast my line in the water. I get pretty excited when the fish nibbles at my bait and pulls the bobber under. I fish just for fun, but there are serious fishermen who really know what they're doing. They know what kind of fish they're after, and they know what it takes to catch them.

In the same way, we need the right bait to reel in souls for the kingdom. Jesus taught us about this in Luke 4:18-19 when he said, "The Spirit of the Lord is upon me, because he hath anointed me to preach the gospel to the poor; he hath sent me to heal the brokenhearted, to preach deliverance to the captives, and recovering of sight to the blind, to set at liberty them that are bruised, To preach the acceptable year of the Lord" (KJV).

What do the poor need to hear? They need to hear that they don't have to be "poor no more." They need to know "my God shall supply all your need according to His riches in glory by Christ Jesus" (Philippians 4:19). The brokenhearted need to know that Jesus mends hearts supernaturally; He replaces sorrow for joy. Captives—those bound by addictions—need to know there's freedom in Jesus. The blind need to hear that Jesus still heals today. And the bruised—or abused physically or emotionally—need to know they don't have to live with physical or emotional pain because Jesus bore their peace of mind just as much as He bore their sins and sicknesses (Isaiah 53:4-5).

Jesus listed these different kinds of "baits" because everybody has a story, and He offers Good News to them all. Whatever they need, God has it. There's nothing too hard for Him.

ACTION ▷ ....

It's time to reel in some fish! If you're serious about fishing for souls, pray this pray aloud with me: *Father, direct me to people who need to hear of Jesus. Teach me to be sensitive to your Spirit and sensitive to people. Open my eyes. Let me not just pray for laborers but be a laborer. I give you my hands, my feet, my ears, my mouth. I'll put my life and my schedule on hold anytime You prompt me. I will yield to Your compassion and long for it to flow out of me in Jesus' name.*

(63) | WHO AND WHAT

Rev. John G. Lake was known for saying that to know God's purpose for your life, it is necessary to know who you are and what you are. Yet, we won't find these answers by the world's standards or in universities and colleges. We find these answers in God.

So look with me at what God says about you:

- You are a child of the Most High God – 1 John 3:1

- You are royalty – 1 Peter 2:9, Revelation 1:6

- You are a new creation – 2 Corinthians 5:17

- You are the righteousness of God in Christ – 2 Corinthians 5:21

- God is in you – Colossians 1:27, 1 John 2:27, 2 Corinthians 6:16, 1 Corinthians 3:16

- You have no limitations – Mark 10:27

- You can do all things through Jesus Christ who strengthens you – Philippians 4:13

- You have the mind of Christ – 1 Corinthians 2:16

- You have power and authority – Luke 10:19

You are to rule and reign in this life – Romans 5:17

ACTION ≫ ....

You've read who and what you are, now declare who and what you are. Read the scriptures aloud several times inserting your name or the word *I*. In fact, God might just lead you to read aloud who and what you are every day for a while.

(64) | POWER AND BOLDNESS

Fisherman can be picky about their rods and reels, and that's a good thing. If you're going to fish, you need the right equipment. Jesus also knew that you would need the right equipment when fishing for souls, so He gave you what you needed: power, boldness and the name above all names.

POWER. In Acts 1:8 Jesus said, "…you shall receive power when the Holy Spirit has come upon you; and you shall be witnesses to Me in Jerusalem, and in all Judea and Samaria, and to the end of the earth." You could read it this way: "You'll receive power after the Holy Ghost has come upon you, and you'll be fishermen in your neighborhood, your job, your city, your state, your nation and the world." How will you get the job done? You will be supernaturally equipped by the Holy Ghost—in His might, power and ability.

We need to overcome the mental block that says, "I'm too shy to talk to people." What's the alternative? To let them go to hell? No. Jesus said we would receive power to witness, so we need to get out of our comfort zone and get busy.

"When will the power come on me?" someone asks. When you need it. The power won't come on you when you're home in bed. It won't come on you while you're watching television or eating dinner. But when you open your mouth to witness, the power will be there. When you open your mouth wide, God will fill it.

BOLDNESS. God has a way of making people bold. Peter denied Jesus three times *before* he received the Holy Ghost, but Acts 4 also tells us about Peter *after* he received the Holy Ghost. Verse 13 says, "Now when they saw the *boldness* of Peter and John…they marveled; and they realized that they had been with Jesus." I love that! Peter and John had been with Jesus, and it showed.

THE NAME OF JESUS. Acts 3 tells how Peter and John were on their way to the temple to pray and passed a beggar who was crippled and sat there most of his life. But that day Peter and John looked at him and said, "Hey man, we don't have money, but here's what we do have! In the name of Jesus, rise up and walk!" He jumped up and began leaping and dancing and praising God.

Later Peter said, "Now, don't think we did this all on our own. God raised from the dead the One you crucified and killed. He rose again, and now it's in His name this man is healed and given soundness in the presence of you all." That's the name above every name: JESUS.

God has given you power and boldness. You have all the equipment you need to reel in fish, and you have a commission to go everywhere doing it. What more do you need?

ACTION ▷ ···

Ask the Holy Spirit to lead you to a person who is ripe for the gospel message today. Who's it going to be?

_____

Love on him or her. Share the truth. First Corinthians 3:6 says some plant, some water and some reap. Do your part!

(65) | JESUS IN ACTION

I t's been said that Smith Wigglesworth prayed daily asking the Lord to lead him to the person closest to eternity so he could witness to that person, and every day he led someone to receive Jesus as Lord and Savior. What a goal! What if every one of us did the same?

Jesus did. Matthew 9:35-36 says, "*Jesus went* about all the cities and villages, teaching in their synagogues, preaching the gospel of the kingdom, and healing every sickness and every disease among the people. But when *He saw* the multitudes, *he was moved with compassion* for them, because they were weary and scattered abroad like sheep having no shepherd."

In fact, Jesus set quite an example for us. He did three important things.

JESUS WENT. The word *went* is a verb that denotes action. In other words, Jesus got up and did something. He didn't sit at home praying for the fish to come to Him. He went where the fish were and used bait to catch them. Fish don't jump in the boat on their own. Most likely, fish will not knock on your front door or wander through your backyard. You will have to go just as Mark 16:15 commanded to win souls. Your world might be your neighborhood, your city, your state or beyond, but there's no question that God wants you fishing.

JESUS SAW. We read in Matthew 9 that Jesus "*saw the multitudes.*" He *really saw* them. It affected Him, and it mattered to Him. Honestly, how many people do we come in contact with on a daily basis that we don't even really see? We walk by people without even noticing them. It could be the person working the counter or the drive-through at Starbucks. It could be the checkout lady at the grocery store. We even say, "Hi! How are you?" but we don't expect much of an answer. We need to get past ourselves—past our busyness and *really see* like Jesus *really saw.*

JESUS WAS MOVED WITH COMPASSION. When Jesus really saw, He was really *"moved with compassion."* He didn't just *have* compassion; it *moved* Him. It resulted in action. Compassion is a supernatural force of love that compels action. When we're full of God and His love, we cannot leave people the way we found them.

 **ACTION** ▷ ....

Be a fisher of men and women today! Ask Jesus to help you *go* where the fish are. Ask Him who's near eternity. Ask Him to help you *really see* the people. Ask Him *to move you with compassion.*

Now *go!*

You'll never be the same again and neither will those you help.

(66) | HOLY GHOST SETUPS

During the ministry of Jesus, we read of many people who touched the heart of Jesus. He loved them. He spoke health and healing to them, and He healed them. Jesus couldn't leave people like He found them, so He brought change to them. That's our job, too.

Let's look at two different Bible accounts so we can better understand something I believe the Spirit of God is speaking to the Church in this hour. First of all, we read in Mark 1, "A man with leprosy came and knelt in front of Jesus, begging to be healed. 'If you are willing, you can heal me and make me clean,' he said. *Moved with compassion, Jesus reached out and touched him.* 'I am willing,' he said. 'Be healed!' Instantly the leprosy disappeared, and the man was healed" (Mark 1:40-42 NLT).

In a second example, let's read about Jesus ministering to two blind men in Matthew 20. "As Jesus and his disciples were leaving Jericho, a large crowd followed him. Two blind men were sitting by the roadside, and when they heard that Jesus was going by, they shouted, 'Lord, Son of David, have mercy on us!' The crowd rebuked them and told them to be quiet, but they shouted all the louder, 'Lord, Son of David, have mercy on us!' Jesus stopped and called them. 'What do you want me to do for you?' he asked. 'Lord,' they answered, 'we want our sight.' *Jesus had compassion on them and touched their eyes.* Immediately they received their sight and followed him" (verses 29-34 NIV).

In both cases, Jesus was the only one who stopped to help. The multitude rebuked the blind men who called out for help, and obviously, most people avoid a man with leprosy. Most people don't want to be bothered. Most people don't want to get involved. Most people believe they are too busy to stop like so many in our society today. And yet, Jesus also was busy, but the difference is that Jesus was busy with His Father's business. Aren't we supposed to be?

I believe throughout our day we come across "Holy Ghost setups" where we're led into situations to help. Many times I know good and well that the situation I've encountered is no accident; the Holy Ghost sent me. These little interruptions, as one minister calls them, usually happen when we're in a hurry on our way somewhere. But Jesus always stopped and always helped. Should we do any less?

In this hour I believe the Spirit of God is endeavoring to open the eyes of the Church. People everywhere are crying, "Can somebody help me? I'm all alone. Does anybody even care?" If we're in tune with the Spirit of God, we will hear this call. We should turn from whatever we're doing and wherever we're going to help. After all, we have an important job on this earth. We are to continue the works of Jesus. We are His ears. We are His eyes. We are His hands. We are His feet.

Without us, Jesus cannot touch a hurting world. But with us, the love of God can reach multitudes.

The love of God is so much more than "I love you. I love peanut butter. I love chocolate." No, it's a supernatural force too big and powerful for the human mind to comprehend. This love and compassion of God will stop you in your tracks and draw you to people who cannot be left like you found them.

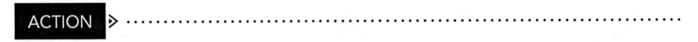

ACTION

Mediate on Romans 5:5 and then follow Jesus' example. Go love on someone today. Ask the Holy Ghost where to go and follow Him. Pray. Encourage. Give. Witness. Bless. Love.

(67) | DIVINE FLOW

In Luke 10 we read the account of the Good Samaritan who stopped to help a man who was mugged on his way from Jerusalem to Jericho. Thieves robbed the man, beat him up, left him dying on the road and ran off. Do we read that before long a priest came by, saw the man and helped him right away? No. A priest came by, but shockingly enough, he crossed to the other side of the road to avoid the man who needed help. Do we read that pretty soon a Levite or religious man came along, saw him and helped? No. He also crossed to the other side so he wouldn't have to walk near him.

"But a certain Samaritan, as he journeyed, came where he was. And when he saw him, he had compassion. So he went to him and bandaged his wounds, pouring on oil and wine; and he set him on his own animal, brought him to an inn, and took care of him. On the next day, when he departed, he took out two denarii, gave them to the innkeeper, and said to him, 'Take care of him; and whatever more you spend, when I come again, I will repay you'" (verses 33-35).

Only the Good Samaritan had compassion on the man. Only the Good Samaritan flowed in the supernatural force of love. He didn't turn away or cross over to the other side. He didn't ignore anything. He nursed the man's wounds and provided transportation for him. He even paid for the man to spend the night in a hotel. He did the best he could to help him.

It's important for us to locate ourselves in this story because the three men who passed by the wounded man are a picture of the body of Christ. God help us to never be the priest or the Levite who doesn't stop but to be the Samaritan who does stop. The truth is, following compassion may not always be easy, but it is always right.

I remember years ago we had a day off and had driven down to the Lake Eufaula area of Oklahoma. It was a no-makeup-hat-kind of day for me, and I really wasn't looking forward to seeing anyone. I just wanted to relax. As the day went on, Mark and I decided to go to Braum's for a milkshake. As I waited in the car while Mark went in, two men came out of the store. It appeared to be a father and son, with the younger man helping an elderly gentleman walk. As they walked near our car and got into theirs, compassion welled up in me. Honestly, at first I thought, *You've got to be kidding me. Not today! No way! I don't want to get out of the car and talk to anybody today. It's my day off.*

About that time, Mark came out, got in the car and turned the key. "Wait!" I said.

"Why?"

"I just feel like I should go talk to that man."

"Well, you better do it then," Mark said.

I knew it was right. I knew missing God would ruin my day; I would have been miserable the rest of the day. So I walked up to their car and tapped on the window. When the elderly man lowered his window, I said, "I was sitting in the next car and saw you come out, and I just felt impressed to ask if I can pray with you."

"Really?" the man said. "I just got released from the hospital, and we're on our way home. I would love for you to pray with me."

He took off the little baseball cap he had on and put it over his heart. We closed our eyes, and I began to pray for the Holy Ghost to strengthen his body and for healing to flow into him from the top of his head to the soles of his feet. I didn't pray long or loud. When I finished, he thanked me. I told him he was very welcome. It's as simple as that. Following compassion doesn't mean booming voices or visions. It doesn't mean handwriting in the sky. Instead, compassion is a divine flow that supernaturally pulls or draws you toward someone. As you follow this flow of compassion, you will be following God.

ACTION ▷ .... ▷

Where are you drawn today? Follow compassion to wherever and to whomever it leads. Ask the Holy Ghost to lead you, and He will.

68 | COMPELLED BY LOVE

For Christ's love compels us....
2 Corinthians 5:14 NIV

Sometimes when compassion moves us to help people, the leading will be overwhelmingly strong, and we know that we know that God wants us to help someone. Other times when compassion moves us, it may be a very subtle and gentle pull. Either way, what a privilege to be compelled by love.

I remember a while back being prompted ever so slightly to help an elderly lady at Walmart. I was picking up some items in the soup section, when the cute little grandma was struggling to reach something on the top shelf. "Ma'am, can I help you?" I asked.

"Why, yes, thank you!" she said. "I want to know how much that item is up there." I don't recall now what the item was, but I do recall that it was $3.49.

"Oh," she said as she turned to walk away.

Immediately, I heard on the inside, "Go back and get that item. Give it to her and give her $20."

At first I thought, *$20?* Then I did just as I heard on the inside. I found her and walked right up and said, "Ma'am, here's that item you wanted, and I want to give you some money to get anything else you might need."

"Why you're part of the family, aren't you?" she smiled and asked.

"Yes, ma'am, I am."

"I knew it when I walked by you," she said.

The truth is, there are all kinds of "fish" out there. Some need salvation. Some need healing. In the case of this little grandma, she needed to know that God would supply all her needs according to His riches in glory by Christ Jesus (Philippians 4:19). It spoke volumes to her that her heavenly Father cared enough to provide her what she needed and bless her with money on top. What a privilege and a joy to live on this earth as an extension of Jesus – His body doing His works.

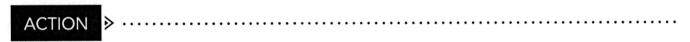

You are the body, and the Head is teaching you to move with Him. Again, today, ask Him where He would have you to go and what He would have you to do. Then follow the Leader.

(69) | FINDING PURPOSE

Do you know why Jesus says that He will make you fishers of men? He says it because it's who He is and what He's all about. Fishing for the souls of men is why He came to this earth. It's His purpose—and yours, too. You're not here by accident. You're not here by happenstance. Jesus has a purpose, and He expects you to be consumed with the same purpose.

Jesus spelled it out in Luke 19 when He said, "For the Son of Man has come to seek and to save that which was lost" (verse 10). That word *lost* means *unable to find one's way*. It means *off course* or *off track and going around in circles*. This world is full of people who are off course, off track and going around in circles. They need Jesus, and He needs us to help them. Jesus has given every one of us the ministry of reconciliation, which is a King James way of saying we need to introduce Jesus Christ to those who are lost and do not yet know Him.

Have you ever been really lost and unable to find your way? It's an awful thing. Yet, we're surrounded by lost people whose eternity ends in hell. We must get off our blessed assurance and find them. If you don't know people who are lost, you need to go fishing for souls.

I remember years ago we were overseas and a pastor's wife said to me, "So I imagine everyone is saved in Tulsa, right?" "No, Ma'am," I said. "We have many Christians in Tulsa, but not everybody is saved." There are many in Tulsa who have yet to hear. There are many in your city who have yet to hear, and we must let the Spirit of God lead us to them. Of course, our close friends should be born again because light and darkness don't mix. However, we can't win lost people for Jesus if we don't know any. We need to be out and about rubbing shoulders with people who need Jesus. Why? That's our purpose; that's the whole reason we're still on this earth.

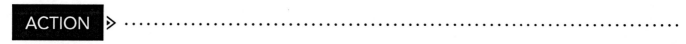

ACTION ▷ ···

Ask the Holy Ghost to lead you to people who are lost, and He will. With different eyes you'll begin to notice the person who checks out your groceries, your waitress, your neighbor, your mechanic, your sales clerk, your mailperson and so many more.

70 | OUR GOD

The god who responds with fire will demonstrate that he is the true God.
1 Kings 18:24 NET

Growing up in Sunday school, I always liked the story of the prophets of Baal who challenged Elijah. Elijah and the prophets of Baal argued over whose god was real and decided to put their gods to the test. "Let's put down a sacrifice, and the god who answers by fire is the real God," Elijah said. "You first!"

The altar was built and the people began crying out, "Baal! Baal! Come on, Baal!" Nothing happened.

"Maybe your god is on vacation," Elijah said. "Maybe your god is taking a nap. Maybe he's checked out." The prophets of Baal got mad and began yelling all the louder. Again, nothing happened, of course.

Finally, Elijah stepped up and said, "Time out. You're done. My turn."

They built their altar of rocks and put down the sacrifice. Then to make sure there would be no question about the results, Elijah said, "Let's use 12 barrels of water to pour on the sacrifice." At his instruction, water was poured over the sacrifice until it was thoroughly saturated.

Elijah stood back and said, "Now let the god that be God answer by fire!" SWOOSH! Fire fell from heaven and consumed up the sacrifice, water and all. All the people—including the prophets of Baal—fell on their faces worshipping the one true God—Almighty God—*our God.*

Nothing is too hard for our God. It doesn't matter what you're facing. Our God is bigger than anything and everything. Trust Him. Delight in Him. Rejoice in Him. And watch Him bring you out victorious.

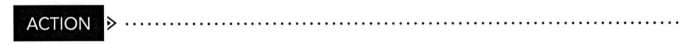

ACTION ▷ ....

Let's brag on OUR GOD today. Tell someone what OUR GOD has done for you. Call someone. Post something on social media. Just brag on God.

(71) | THE WAY WE WERE

Marriage is a God-idea that God set in motion from the beginning, and His plan is that great marriages become greater, good marriages become better and bad marriages become good. On the other hand, it seems like the devil has targeted an all-out war on marriages today, so wise up and devil-proof your marriage.

The reality is that marriages may be made in heaven, but couples must walk them out on earth. The best way to do that is to keep God in the middle of the marriage and keep alive what brought you together in the first place.

As a pastor I've heard many people say, "There's just no spark in my marriage anymore. Whatever was there is all gone now." Here's my response. If your relationship worked at one point, it can work again. It all comes down to good information and good decisions.

Every marriage encounters speed bumps and conflict along the way. Yet, no matter how long or short you've been married, it's important to ask yourself on a regular basis, *Who is the person I fell in love with? What drew me to him or her?*

"Why do I need to ask those questions?"

Because it's important that you don't forget the answers.

Time and even challenges over the years tend to blur the realities that brought you together. Worse yet, sometimes our lives get so busy and crazy that we get sidetracked and our focus becomes fuzzy and cluttered. Your spouse may not look the same. (Most likely, you don't either!) Your spouse may not act the same. (Most likely, you don't either!) So we lose sight of who and what we fell in love with in the beginning, but remembering those qualities infuses your marriage with strength, stirs up feelings and restores your vision.

ACTION ⊳ ···

Jot down 10 things that caused you to fall in love with your spouse. Remember the first smile or first kiss you shared. Remember when you became engaged. Then maybe—just maybe—go read the list to your spouse.

1._____

2._____

3._____

4._____

5._____

6._____

7._____

8._____

9._____

10._____

(72) | MATING SEASON

In this day and age, some people don't speak too well of marriage. I've even heard young people say, "I might not want to get married. It might box me in!" But I don't agree with that thinking at all. Marriage doesn't trap people in; it blocks trouble out.

I heard it said once that marriage is not a fence to trap you in, but a guardrail to protect you. How very true. God planned from the beginning that each of us would find this safety, companionship and trust in marriage. It's what God intends marriage to be.

God Himself said it's not good for man to be alone, which means it isn't good for woman either. God craved fellowship and companionship and designed you to crave it also. God created Adam so the two of them could enjoy fellowship spirit to spirit. Then God created Adam and Eve so they could fellowship with one another on three levels—spirit, soul and body. I believe the happy person has both relationships—deep, intimate fellowship with God and deep, intimate fellowship as a couple. That's God's plan.

So often people think a mate is the answer to all their problems, but it's not. Even the apostle Paul said it's OK to be single if we choose to be. Bottom line, our completeness doesn't come from another individual but from the Lord. When we get wrapped up in Him, He will in turn give us the desires of our heart (Psalm 37:4). If your desire is to be married, put your trust in Him and watch Him bring it to pass.

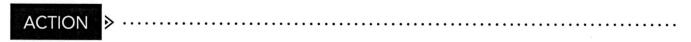

ACTION ▷ ....

If you desire a mate, ask yourself this question: Have I actually told God this is the desire of my heart and put my trust in Him to bring it about? If you have, be encouraged. He's working on it even now.

If you have not, then pray with me now: *Father, Your Word says that You give us the desires of our heart, and I desire a mate. I believe You have given me this desire, and I trust You to bring it about. Thank You for finding the best spouse in the world for me. Thank You for divine connections and supernatural setups that bring us together to live Your plan for our lives.*

Write yourself a note below about praying this prayer today—a note that someday you might want to show your spouse.

_____

_____

_____

_____

_____

(73) | MARRIED ON PURPOSE

When we get married, our order of priorities should be God first and spouse second, but after couples have children, the spouse unfortunately sometimes slides to third, fourth or even fifth place. Some folks think, *That's the way it ought to be. After all, we created these children, and we need to invest in their lives.* Here's some good advice: Don't let *your* priorities slide.

There's no question that you must invest in the lives of your children; they are a high priority. Yet, the best thing you can do for your children is to love your spouse—*really love* your spouse. Your children need to see your marriage strong. They need to see you love God and love your spouse. It makes them feel secure.

Another reason your children need to see a strong marriage is because what you live is what they inherit. Day in and day out you're showing your children *how* to be married, and they're watching. If you have a bad marriage, your children probably will have a bad marriage, too. I can almost guarantee it. On the other hand, if you will demonstrate a good marriage, they will learn from you and have one like it. It's just the way it works.

I know a case right now where a couple had been married for more than 30 years and had three grown children. Eventually, the couple split up saying they should never should have married in the first place. After 30 years together, I highly doubt that. I think it's more likely that the couple invested so much into their children over the years that when the kids left there was nothing left between them. The couple probably didn't even know each other anymore. They didn't remember why they got married, and they had gone two separate ways under one roof.

The problem was that they did not remain best friends or sweethearts, and it shouldn't be that way. Don't let it be that way for you. Keep your marriage strong by spending time together. It puts a stop to sliding priorities. It keeps the friendship and the romance strong. Actually, spending quality time together focused on each other fixes a lot of things. As a couple and as pastors, Mark and I recommend couples schedule one date night a week.

"But we just don't have money to go out on dates," somebody might say. Make two peanut butter sandwiches and go to the park. Take a walk around the neighborhood. Take a drive. Go have coffee. Just hang out together. Pursue each other. Pick up 99 cent cards for each other. Write sticky notes and leave them around the bedroom. Text your spouse. Don't let the flames go out. Don't lose the spark. Fan the flames.

Here's the truth of the matter: Most marriages don't end in a surprise explosion or a sudden blow out. Most marriages end with a slow and steady leak. Then one day, before you know it, the couple says, "What happened to our marriage? Where did it go?"

Be married on purpose.

It's a lifetime commitment that requires lifetime romance. It requires maximum effort day in and day out. Don't ever think, *We're past all that. We've been married more than one year, or more than five years or more than 10 years.* Make sure you never get passed the friendship and the romance.

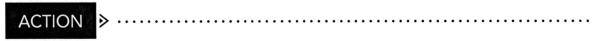

Spend time together. Do something fun. Do something romantic.

Pick three of the suggestions below and do them this week:

1. Send a text or buy a card!

2. Buy him/her a favorite candy, make a favorite meal or make reservations!

3. Compliment your spouse every day this week!

4. Give a gift – small, large or just thoughtful!

5. Get your spouse *really* talking and *really* listen!

6. Take a long walk together and leave the dog and the children home.

(74) | OPPOSITES ATTRACT

When I went to Bible school in my early 20s, I lived with five other girls in a three-bedroom townhouse. We all got along beautifully, and I never had a single argument with any of them. In fact, I never had an argument with anyone on the face of the earth until Mark and I got married. But the truth is, every married couple on earth has disagreements; there's no way around it. No matter how in love a couple is, they won't see eye-to-eye on everything because they are two people blending into one. The word *blend* is the key.

Couples, don't throw in the towel saying, "This marriage is never going to work! I'm done! I quit!" Just keep blending. Understand your differences. And appreciate them.

All you have to do is watch a "chick flick" together and all the differences will be clear. The wife will probably sniffle through the whole thing while the husband would rather watch guns shooting with army trucks, aliens or cowboys riding off into the sunset. Girls want love stories. Guys want heroes and conquests. But here's the point. You can either get aggravated at the differences, or you can learn to appreciate them. The truth be told, the differences were there when you met. In fact, I heard it put this way: Opposites attract before marriage. Opposites irritate after marriage.

So what will you do about the differences? Should you try to change your spouse? No. Appreciate the differences. Laugh about them. Recognize you both bring differences to the relationship. If you were rubber stamp copies of each other, you would be bored with each other. Actually, it's the differences that make things work. So let your differences complete you and complement you. Choose to let your differences make you a stronger unit.

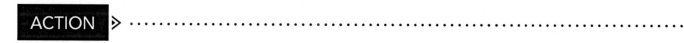

ACTION ▷ ....

Name five ways you and your spouse are opposites and how together it makes you stronger:

HUSBAND TRAITS	WIFE TRAITS	HOW TOGETHER WE'RE BETTER

(75) | GOLDEN RULE

If you can get a couple to walk in the God-kind of love, they can have a happily ever after every time because love never fails. On the other hand, if you've been in a marriage that didn't work and it ended in divorce, there's no condemnation. It is not the unpardonable sin. If you've been divorced, it's in the past now. Don't beat yourself up and don't let anybody else beat you up. Just decide to rise up and go on with life. Determine that your future will be better and brighter.

When we talk about love and marriage, it's never meant as condemnation for unsuccessful relationships. What we're doing is getting out our swords of the Word and the Spirit to devil-proof our futures. Let's face facts. Love never gives up, but it doesn't come without a struggle sometimes. Love doesn't just ride along merrily through life with everything all wonderful. Love encounters its share of speed bumps and obstacles along the way, but love *never* fails.

As born-again Christians, the love of God has been "…poured out in our hearts by the Holy Spirit…" (Romans 5:5). So we've got the equipment inside us to win every time if we'll yield to the inside instead of the outside. But the love of God is not a passive, ooey-gooey-here-today-gone-tomorrow emotion that's up and down. The love of God is a choice. It's constant. It believes the best of every person. It doesn't keep score of wrongs. It's patient and kind. It endures long. It doesn't fly off the handle. It's not touchy, fretful or resentful. When somebody irritates you—spouse, friend, child, coworker or whomever—pull on that love inside you. Let it rise up. Love can take the sting out of all those other emotions.

Love races to see who can say "I'm sorry!" first. Every disagreement is not another opportunity to place blame on somebody. Don't get caught up in, "Well, it was your fault!" "No, it was clearly your fault." Who cares? Does it really matter who started it? Just end it. If you really want any relationship to work, it's love that will make it all go around.

Actually, have you ever been in a disagreement when all of the sudden you can't even remember what started it or what you were arguing over? Usually it all comes down to stress or pressure or being tired. Usually it all comes down to nitpicky little things that don't matter at all.

Let's purpose to live by the Golden Rule. We all know the Golden Rule, but consider it in light of marriage: Do unto your mate as you would have your mate do unto you. If married couples live by that rule, they'll be trying to outdo each other. It's a seedtime and harvest principle that will cause you to reap the happy marriage you want. There's no better place to sow than in your own marriage and family.

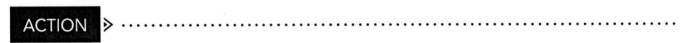

ACTION ▷ ·

Promise yourself here and now that the very next time you find yourself in a disagreement, you will refuse to participate in placing blame. You will be the first person to say you're sorry, and you will be the first person to "get glad in the same pants you got mad in." Write down today's date just to remind yourself of your promise.

⑦⑥ | STRIFE OUT

If we're going to live *The God Life*—and live beyond the ordinary—we're going to have to love beyond the ordinary. We'll have to love God's way, which means walking in the God-kind of love and locking strife out of our lives and our homes.

A home with yelling, shouting, strife and discord is not a home; it's a house at best. Every member of the family needs to make a quality decision to race each other to stop discord from starting. Be the first to end it when it does start and be the first to say I'm sorry. Sure, there will be disagreements. It's a normal part of living, but it doesn't have to mean yelling, shouting, strife and discord.

Ephesians 4:29-32 says this: "Let no corrupt word proceed out of your mouth, but what is good for necessary edification, that it may impart grace to the hearers. And do not grieve the Holy Spirit of God, by whom you were sealed for the day of redemption. Let all bitterness, wrath, anger, clamor, and evil speaking be put away from you, with all malice. And be kind to one another, tenderhearted, forgiving one another, even as God in Christ forgave you."

The Amplified Bible translates the passage this way: "Let no foul or polluting language, nor evil word nor unwholesome or worthless talk [ever] come out of your mouth, but only such [speech] as is good and beneficial to the spiritual progress of others, as is fitting to the need and the occasion, that it may be a blessing and give grace (God's favor) to those who hear it. And do not grieve the Holy Spirit of God…. Let all bitterness and indignation and wrath (passion, rage, bad temper) and resentment (anger, animosity) and quarreling (brawling, clamor, contention) and slander (evil-speaking, abusive or blasphemous language) be banished from you, with all malice (spite, ill will, or baseness of any kind). And become useful and helpful and kind to one another, tenderhearted (compassionate, understanding, loving-hearted), forgiving one another [readily and freely], as God in Christ forgave you.

The Message translation says, "Watch the way you talk. Let nothing foul or dirty come out of your mouth. Say only what helps, each word a gift. Don't grieve God. Don't break his heart. His Holy Spirit, moving and breathing in you, is the most intimate part of your life, making you fit for himself. Don't take such a gift for granted. Make a clean break with all cutting, backbiting, profane talk. Be gentle with one another, sensitive. Forgive one another as quickly and thoroughly as God in Christ forgave you."

Words matter, so make each word a gift as we just read. If you start to make a comment you know will cut, instead cut yourself off. The old saying, "Sticks and stones may break my bones, but words can never hurt me" is not true. Words can hurt and pierce to the very core. They can break hearts and end relationships. Think twice about your words because once they're out there, there's no taking them back. The Bible is very clear about the fact that we do have control over what comes out of our mouths. It's a choice. So we need to make sure our words are sweet because we may have to eat them.

On the other side of the conversation, love never gets offended. Love is the high road; offense is the easy road. Which road will you take? You cannot afford to have offense anywhere near you—not near your house or your spouse. It always boils down to a choice. So, just say *no* to offense.

ACTION ⟫ ···

Purpose that you will walk in love today and every day. Decide to make each word a gift. Decide to never go to bed mad. Refuse to be offended and refuse to offend. To live beyond the ordinary, you must love beyond the ordinary.

(77) | LOVE MEANS SAYING SORRY

Loving God's way means being the first one to apologize, even to the point of taking the blame when we're not sure we deserve it. When it comes right down to it, very seldom will any two people agree on who really deserves the blame in a disagreement. So the solution is to handle the situation like Jesus handled us.

Jesus didn't deserve our blame, but He took it just the same. He took it because He loved us. Now we're supposed to love like He loved because His love is in us. Think about His kind of love. Jesus not only took our sins on the cross, but He took our blame for all the dumb things we did in life. He went to the cross as our substitute when we deserved to go. In light of that, we ought to be able to say in any disagreement, "This is not worth arguing about. This is not worth debating."

Sometimes folks in our church think Mark and I are the perfect couple, and we have been blessed with a wonderful marriage for more than 30 years. But the truth is, no one has a wonderful marriage without work. Mark and I are actually two very strong personalities, and we disagree like everyone else. But even just walking in the love of God, we get to a point where we say, "It's not worth taking hours to decide who started this disagreement or whose fault it is." It's so much better to race to be the first one to say, "I'm sorry. It's my fault. I don't even know where it started."

I remember talking one night with our elderly neighbors who had been married more than 75 years. As we visited with them, I asked, "Uncle Johnny, Aunt Ruthie, what's the key to your long, happy marriage?" Without any hesitation, they both answered, "*Never* go to bed mad!"

Ephesians 4 tells us the same thing: "'Don't sin by letting anger control you.' Don't let the sun go down while you are still angry" (Ephesians 4:26 NLT). "Why is going to bed mad such a big deal?" somebody asks. Because if we go to bed mad, we wake up mad. We create an atmosphere of anger, and we learn to live in it. We get used to it, and we open our homes to strife "and every evil work." God has a much better way!

 **ACTION** ▷ ···

First John 3:20 says you can have confidence before God unless your heart condemns you. So, let's get real here. Is your heart talking to you? Do you need to say "I'm sorry?" Do you need to forgive somebody? Do you need to let go of anger? Mark 11:25 says, "Whenever you stand praying, if you have anything against anyone, forgive him and let it drop (leave it, let it go), in order that your Father Who is in heaven may also forgive you your [own] failings and shortcomings and let them drop" (AMP).

⑦⑧ | INFLUENCED BY WORDS

We're all influenced by the power of words spoken to us and over us. The words our parents or mentors speak influence us greatly just as the words we speak over our children and grandchildren influence them positively or negatively. The word *influence,* according to The Merriam-Webster Dictionary, means *the power to sway or cause a change in character, thought or action.* That is why the influence of words needs to be used wisely.

For example, if you tell your child, he or she is stupid and will never amount to anything, the child probably won't amount to anything. Hurtful words will influence the child's self-esteem, opinions and choices. The best thing parents can do is speak the Word over their children just as God has spoken over us. We need to put the Word to work *for* our children and *in* our children.

Put the Word to work for your children*.* It's never too early or too late to start. Build them up. Thank God that they are born again and filled with the Spirit at an early age and walking with God all the days of their lives. Thank God that your children fulfill God's highest plan and purpose for their lives. Thank Him that they always have good friends, good teachers, good schools and good jobs. Thank God that your children marry good spouses and that their every need is met—spirit, soul and body.

Put the Word in your children so they will work the Word*.* Teach your children what the Word says about them until they know it—and say it—for themselves. Listen to them quote the scriptures until you can hear it spoken in faith from their hearts.

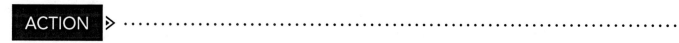

ACTION ▷ ⋯⋯⋯⋯⋯⋯⋯⋯⋯⋯⋯⋯⋯⋯⋯⋯⋯⋯⋯⋯⋯⋯⋯⋯⋯

Below are important scriptures that will put the Word to work for and in your children. Confess these scriptures daily over your children and encourage them to do the same. These words will carry a powerful influence over the little loved ones in your life.

- You can do all things through Jesus Christ who strengthens you (Philippians 4:13).

- You are safe and protected at all times in all things (Psalm 91).

- Put God first and everything else will be added to you (Matthew 6:33).

- Greater is He that's in you than he that's in the world (1 John 4:4).

- You have the mind of Christ (1 Corinthians 2:16).

- Just as God gave the Hebrew children "knowledge and skill in all learning and wisdom," He will give it to you. The Hebrew children were 10 times smarter, and you can be, too. (Daniel 1:17, 20).

- You will have wisdom more than your teachers because God is with you (Psalm 119:99-100).

- Everything you put your hand to will prosper (Deuteronomy 28:8).

- You will be satisfied with a long life (Psalm 91:16).

- Surely goodness and mercy will follow you all the days of your life (Psalm 23:6).

(79) | PRETTY IS AS PRETTY DOES

My sweet momma was the queen of quotes, and I got some real gems from her as I grew up. Even though she's stepped over to heaven, every now and then, another one of her quotes will come to mind. One of them she used to tell me often is that "pretty is as pretty does."

Her point was that how a person looks physically is only a small part of the person's beauty because what really determines beauty is a person's heart. Beauty on the outside can come from genetics or bottles, jars and tubes, but pretty on the inside is a whole different story.

The apostle Peter was known for his quotes, too, and here's what he said about beauty. "Don't be concerned about the outward beauty of fancy hairstyles, expensive jewelry, or beautiful clothes. You should clothe yourselves instead with the beauty that comes from within, the unfading beauty of a gentle and quiet spirit, which is so precious to God" (1 Peter 3:3-4 NLT).

Paul also talked about a pretty—or handsome—wardrobe and said, "You're done with that old life. It's like a filthy set of ill-fitting clothes you've stripped off and put in the fire. Now you're dressed in a new wardrobe. Every item of your new way of life is custom-made by the Creator, with his label on it. All the old fashions are now obsolete. Words like Jewish and non-Jewish, religious and irreligious, insider and outsider, uncivilized and uncouth, slave and free, mean nothing. From now on everyone is defined by Christ, everyone is included in Christ. So, chosen by God for this new life of love, dress in the wardrobe God picked out for you: compassion, kindness, humility, quiet strength, discipline. Be even-tempered, content with second place, quick to forgive an offense. Forgive as quickly and completely as the Master forgave you. And regardless of what else you put on, wear love. It's your basic, all-purpose garment. Never be without it" (Colossians 3:9-14 The Message).

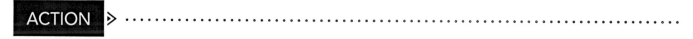

ACTION ▷ ....

Just like you take a look in the mirror after getting dressed, take a good long look in the mirror of God's Word (James 1:22-25) as a standard of how pretty or handsome you are on the *inside*. Make a few notes below as the Word and the Holy Ghost point out a few things to you.

_____

_____

_____

_____

_____

(80) | FAITH CONTAINERS

Another saying my momma quoted countless times as I was growing up is this: "If you don't have something good to say, then don't say anything at all." Actually, it wasn't until I first heard Word of Faith teaching in 1974 that I realized what really good—and really scriptural—advice she gave me.

Throughout the Bible we're told that our words matter a great deal to God. Proverbs 18:21 says we have the power of life and death in our tongues. Matthew 12:36 says we will give account for idle words in the day of judgment. Luke 6:45 says out of the abundance of the heart we speak. James 3 says that we can change the course of our lives with words like a rudder changes the course of a ship. Hebrews 11:3 tells us the worlds were framed by faith, and we frame our own worlds by faith because the God-kind of faith operates by *believing and saying*.

Believing is as easy as breathing for a believer. Romans 10:17 says that "faith comes by hearing, and hearing the word of God." If it's a strain or a struggle to believe, we simply have not heard enough of God's Word. Then 2 Corinthians 4:13 says, "Since we have the same spirit of faith, according to what is written, 'I believed and therefore I spoke,' we also believe and therefore speak." Words are containers of our faith, and as we speak them, we release faith to work for us.

Jesus Himself said *saying* is pretty important: "For assuredly, I say to you, whoever *says* to this mountain, 'Be removed and be cast into the sea,' and does not doubt in his heart, but believes that those things he *says* will be done, he will have whatever he *says*" (Mark 11:23). Did you notice that Jesus referred to saying three times more than believing? Why? It's because most of us need to focus three times more on what we say than what we believe. So make your words containers of faith and start speaking to mountains!

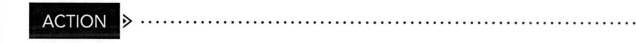

ACTION ▷ ··

Look up these scriptures and make yourself some notes!

Psalm 107:20 | Proverbs 4:22 | Proverbs 12:18 | Proverbs 6:2 | Proverbs 21:23 | Proverbs 13:3 | Proverbs 30:32 | Matthew 21 | Mark 11 | Revelation 12:11

_____

_____

_____

_____

_____

(81) | BAD NEWS

Strife and offense are bad news. They can kill relationships, friendships or even churches, and they open the door to the devil to ruin your life. Second Timothy 2:23-26 tells us what to do about it: "...Don't get involved in foolish, ignorant arguments that only start fights. A servant of the Lord must not quarrel but must be kind to everyone, be able to teach, and be patient with difficult people. Gently instruct those who oppose the truth. Perhaps God will change those people's hearts, and they will learn the truth. Then they will come to their senses and escape from the devil's trap. For they have been held captive by him to do whatever he wants" (NLT).

Face facts. The devil has traps set for you, and it's by your words that you fall into those traps or avoid them. You need to avoid strife like the plague. In fact, second-hand strife is just as deadly as second-hand smoke. It destroys everything it touches, so be known as the person who just says no to strife—no time, no how, no way.

"People should just learn to get over things," somebody might say. It's true that people should refuse offense. Psalm 119:165 says, "Great peace have they which love thy law: and nothing shall offend them" (KJV). At the same time, that doesn't give you a license to go around hurting people with your words. You've probably heard the old saying, "Sticks and stones may break my bones, but words will never hurt me." That's just plain not true. Words can hurt a whole lot.

So choose to be a peacemaker. Choose to build people up with your words—not tear them down. Minister grace to the hearer. Comfort them. Help them. Leave them better off for having known you.

ACTION ▷ ···

Run through your mind various conversations you had during the past week and determine if any of them should have been edited. As you recognize where change is needed, you'll be empowered to change.

_____

_____

(82) | FOLLOW THE LEADER

Most people will never hear God speak in a booming, audible voice, but God leads and guides us just the same. Our whole walk with God begins and ends with being able to follow the Leader. In fact, the number one way God leads His children is through the inward witness. It's a peaceful, velvety feeling on the inside that we could describe as *a prompt, a leading, a hunch, an urge or a nudge.* As we come to know God better through reading His Word and praying in the Spirit, it becomes easier and easier to recognize His leading.

For example, if you were to blindfold me and put me in a room with my husband and 300 talking people, I could still find him. It might take me a few minutes, but I could find my way to Mark's voice and pick it out of a crowd because I hear it all the time. I *know* his voice. This is the same level we need to reach in recognizing God's direction.

There are many opinions in this world—our opinions, family opinions, friend opinions, expert opinions and on and on. Yet, God's direction is the one we cannot afford to miss because it's the one that keeps us on the right road. God is the One who tells us when we need to turn, stop or even change directions through life's decisions. It's His leading that will prompt us by saying, "Don't marry him or her." "Don't buy that house or car." "Do go after a certain job because it's the best one for you." God is willing to guide us every step of the way through life.

Never wonder for a single second if God's plans for you are good. Trust me, they are. The life God has planned for you is better than you ever dreamed possible. His plans will satisfy you to the fullest and plant you smack dab in the middle of everything you were destined to be and do. You have God's Word on it. Jeremiah 29:11 says, "I know what I'm doing. I have it all planned out—plans to take care of you, not abandon you, plans to give you the future you hope for" (The Message). That's the God you and I serve—the One who wants all of us traveling the road to success.

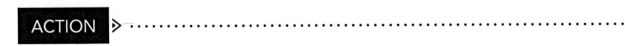

ACTION ▷ ···

What are some areas in life where you need direction?

_____

_____

_____

_____

_____

Meditate on these scriptures:

John 10:27 | Romans 8:14 | Proverbs 20:27 | 1 John 2:27 | John 16:13 | 1 Corinthians 2:9 | Ephesians 2:10
Psalm 37:23 | Proverbs 19:21 | Psalm 37:4 | Proverbs 20:5

(83) | ROAD TO SUCCESS

Where are you headed in life? How will you end up? No matter how you answer those questions, there's something important you need to know: Success in life is not up to God nearly as much as it's up to *you* and *me*. The choices are ours to make, so I'm thankful God gave us a guidebook called the Bible to help us live on this earth. If we hold tightly to it, it will bring us success in every area of life.

One of the best instructions I've found in my guidebook is in Proverbs 4:

Listen, friends, to some fatherly advice; sit up and take notice so you'll know how to live. I'm giving you good counsel; don't let it go in one ear and out the other. When I was a boy at my father's knee, the pride and joy of my mother, He would sit me down and drill me: 'Take this to heart. Do what I tell you—live! Sell everything and buy Wisdom! Forage for Understanding! Don't forget one word! Don't deviate an inch! (verses 1-5 The Message).

Dear friend, take my advice; it will add years to your life. I'm writing out clear directions to Wisdom Way, I'm drawing a map to Righteous Road. I don't want you ending up in blind alleys, or wasting time making wrong turns. Hold tight to good advice; don't relax your grip. Guard it well—your life is at stake! Don't take Wicked Bypass; don't so much as set foot on that road. Stay clear of it; give it a wide berth. Make a detour and be on your way... (verses 10-15 The Message).

Dear friends, listen well to my words; tune your ears to my voice. Keep my message in plain view at all times. Concentrate! Learn it by heart! Those who discover these words live, really live; body and soul, they're bursting with health. Keep vigilant watch over your heart; that's where life starts.... Keep your eyes straight ahead; ignore all sideshow distractions. Watch your step and the road will stretch out smooth before you... (verses 20-23, 25-26 The Message).

The chapter we just read is an instruction for life. It's not only something we should live by, but if we pay attention to its words we'll also discover how to *really* live. Solomon, who wrote the Book of Proverbs, wasn't talking about a life where we barely get by or life as usual. No—he was talking about the kind of life that God planned for His kids. You see, the Bible calls God's children a chosen people, and there's no way we're supposed to be like everybody else. We're supposed to be in this world but not of it. God has set a standard in His Word for us to walk by and live by that put us on the road to a good life, a divine life, a really abundant life. He wants us experiencing *The God Life—living way beyond the ordinary*. So grab hold of it and don't let go.

ACTION ▷ ··

Ask yourself a few questions about how often and how much time you spend in God's Word. The answers are only for you to see.

1. Do I spend time in God's Word daily? _____

2. How much time daily? _____

3. How much time weekly?_____

4. Has this proven to be enough to keep me full of the Word and strong in faith?_____
    If you liked your answers, great! If you did not, then here's one more question:_____

5. So what will I do about it? What's my new plan for time in God's Word? _____

_____

_____

_____

_____

_____

Don't let a day go by without God's Word in your life. *Make time* for it!

(84) | LISTEN WELL

Dear friends, listen well to my words; tune your ears to my voice.
Proverbs 4:20 The Message

There's a big difference between listening and hearing. Ask any wife! Most wives are married to husbands who at least occasionally demonstrate the difference between listening and hearing. I laugh about this, but there are times when I'm talking away, and Mark is sitting right across the table from me hearing every word but not listening to a single word.

I saw a commercial on TV awhile back that really makes the point. I don't even remember what they were advertising. The husband was sitting at the kitchen table reading his newspaper when the wife walked into the room with a new dress on and asked, "Honey, does this dress make me look fat?" Still reading but never looking up, the husband says, "Absolutely, honey. Absolutely!" The wife stormed out of the room, and the guy was in big trouble, of course. While it's funny when I joke about husbands doing it, it's not funny when wives do it either. It's not funny when anybody does it, and it's especially not funny when we do the same thing to God.

The problem is that some people go to church, sit on the pew, and hear and hear, but never really listen. God knows that, which is why He said, "Listen well to my words! Tune your ears to my voice!" Whether you realize it or not, you're already skilled at tuning in and out voices. You do it every time you go to a restaurant. You tune out background noise, while tuning in the person you want to hear. Train yourself to do the same thing with the voice of God. Block out everything else. Tune your ear to what God is saying because it will lead you to success.

ACTION ▷ ···

Spend some time talking to the Lord today, and then spend an equal amount of time listening. Prayer should be a *conversation* between you and God!

(85) | BY HEART

Dear friends, listen well to my words; tune your ears to my voice. Keep my message in plain view at all times. Concentrate! Learn it by heart! Those who discover these words live, really live; body and soul, they're bursting with health. Keep vigilant watch over your heart; that's where life starts…. Keep your eyes straight ahead; ignore all sideshow distractions. Watch your step and the road will stretch out smooth before you….
Proverbs 4:20-23, 25-26 The Message

Mark often teaches that we should stick with the Word until it sticks with us, and the scripture above really tells us the same thing. Notice these phrases in particular: "*Keep my message in plain view at all times. Concentrate! Learn it by heart!*"

Growing up in Sunday school, I remember we had weekly memory verses, and the truths I buried in my heart shaped my life. These days no one assigns you and me memory verses, so we better do it for ourselves. The truth is, we need God's words memorized on the inside of us to live a life beyond the ordinary. We need to have God's Words engraved in our heart because it will enable us to live *The God Life* of success. God's Word will make every one of us healthy, wealthy and wise.

When God thinks something is important, He doesn't just throw it out once in the Bible and hope we don't skip that chapter. He makes His principles clear over and over like He does the principle of meditating in Joshua 1:8 that says, "Study this Book of Instruction continually. Meditate on it day and night so you will be sure to obey everything written in it. Only then will you prosper and succeed in all you do" (NLT).

If you want guaranteed success in your life, Joshua is telling you how to get it: *Meditate the Word.* How? Think about it, ponder it, dwell on it, and roll it over and over and over. Find a verse that applies to whatever situation you're in right now—whether you need healing, finances or direction—and meditate on it. Don't just read it, skip over the parts that challenge you, go your way, and never think about it again. Let the Word drop from your head to your heart. When that happens, a verse will become life to you. You think about it and apply it to your situation.

For example, when symptoms attack my body, the verse I meditate on more times than not is Romans 8:11 that says, "If the Spirit of Him who raised Jesus from the dead dwells in you, He who raised Christ from the dead will also give life to your mortal bodies through His Spirit who dwells in you." I begin to talk to my body and say, "Body, the same Spirit that raised Jesus from the dead dwells in me. Therefore, that same Spirit is quickening, making alive, my mortal flesh. Therefore, body, you have to line up with the Word." It comes out from my heart because it has dropped from my head to my heart. You couldn't talk me out of it if you tried, and that's what happens when you meditate. The Word becomes a part of you. If you need success in your health, business, finances, direction or even relationships, find out what God has said about your situation and meditate on it.

ACTION ⟫ ···

Ask the Holy Ghost to help you find a scripture today that applies to situations you face, and write it below. Above all, quote it throughout the day and keep on quoting it in faith until it delivers victory in your life.

_____

_____

_____

_____

_____

(86) | UP THE HILL AND DOWN

The world has distorted the meaning of *success*. It isn't about how much money we have in the bank or fancy job titles. Actually, according to The Amerian Heritage Dictionary, *success* means the *achievement of something desired, planned or attempted.* Now that's more like it! I guarantee that many of us have desires hidden in our hearts that we haven't told anyone. Perhaps they're things we've seen ourselves doing, or perhaps they're plans God is yet to bring to pass. The achievement of God's plans for our lives *is* what success is really all about.

The words *achievement of something attempted* prompt me with a flashback to the first time I went skiing. I'm a southern girl who married a northerner from Michigan, and it wasn't long after we were married that a couple of his friends invited us to go skiing. As Mark and his friends headed out to ski, I suggested I would watch for a while. Really, I stood at the bottom of the hill watching for a long time—a really, really long time. I remember thinking, *I've watched so long now, my feet are numb.*

Finally, I tried to ski and failed big time. Let's say it wasn't a pretty picture. The instructors may still remember me. They told me, "Skiing is so easy. Just grab hold of the rope, stand up, and it will pull you up." I thought, *Well, I can do that!* So I grabbed hold of the rope, but somehow my body ended up *over* the rope. It drug me up the hill slowly enough that all the people behind me were piling up. It was horrible! Even my husband acted like he didn't know me that day, but I informed him that I was from the South where we enjoy beaches with our toes buried in warm sand. Skiing wasn't for me, and it wasn't even a pleasant memory. I had attempted skiing and failed big time.

Before long we traveled to Colorado where we were invited to go skiing yet again. *Oh boy!* I thought, *not this again.* Most people on the slopes acted like they were having a lot of fun, while I was thinking, *Why would anyone want to slide around on a skinny stick and be cold on top of it?* Growing up in the South, this made absolutely no sense to me. But it's important in life not to be a quitter, so I tried skiing again. That time it was much better. Now, mind you, I'm not what you would call an expert skier, but I got up the hill and got down. I achieved something, and I was happy. It made no difference to me that it was a beginner's slope or a bunny hill because all I cared about was that I got up and got down. Success was mine. And, if you attempt or re-attempt something hard, you'll know sweet success, too.

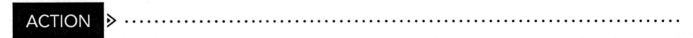

ACTION

If you've let fear rob you of success in an area, admit it. Then tackle it. Whatever it is, you may not become an expert, but you can become successful!

(87) | SWEET SUCCESS

Do you have things in your heart you've been too chicken to try? You might wonder, *If I step out and attempt this I might fail!* So what? If you fail, just get up and do it again until you don't fail. Smith Wigglesworth once said, "The mark of a successful man is one who gets up one more time than he falls down."

One thing for sure, success will *never* happen until you attempt to do something.

God wants your whole life and every decision in it to be successful. He wants you to have the desires of your heart. He wants you to achieve those desires and plans that He's given you for your life. But as long as you're sitting and singing the song, "I shall not be, I shall not be moved," you sure won't be. Don't let that be your theme song. Your job is to hear the voice of God—be willing and obedient—and be on the move. It won't work to be sitting down doing nothing and be headed for success at the same time.

God will always give you plans and dreams bigger than you are, and if you are going to live *The God Life* and walk with Him, you'll have to step up your game and follow the Leader. Don't ever doubt that God wants success for you. Don't ever doubt that you can do whatever He puts in your heart because He said you can do all things through Jesus Christ who strengthens you.

God wants success for you, but *you* make that happen by meditating in the Word and doing what it says. God's Word will always lead you to success.

ACTION ▷ ···

It's time to admit a dream in your heart that's actually scared you. _____. There it is in black and white. Now it's time to take one step toward that dream. Then all you have to do is keep on walking. You can do it. So just do it!

(88) | THRILL TO GOD'S WORD

How well God must like you—you don't hang out at Sin Saloon, you don't slink along Dead-End Road, you don't go to Smart-Mouth College. Instead you thrill to God's Word, you chew on Scripture day and night. You're a tree replanted in Eden, bearing fresh fruit every month, never dropping a leaf, always in blossom.
Psalm 1:1-3 The Message

Let it be said of every one of us that we thrill to God's Word—that we love it and live by it. The prophet Jeremiah said something similar when he said, "Your words were found, and I ate them, And Your word was to me the joy and rejoicing of my heart" (Jeremiah 15:16). In other words, we need to "eat" the Word, absorb it and let it get into our system.

When you get hungry, don't go to the refrigerator; pull out your Bible instead. Thrill to God's Word by meditating on it day and night. Putting God's Word first place doesn't leave any time to meditate on things that don't deserve our focus.

You see, the devil attacks the mind and his attacks almost always come first in the form of a thought. Then it's your choice what you do with those thoughts. Do you take them and make them your own by thinking about them over and over? Or do you kick them out of your mind?

The devil never plays fair. He often comes with thoughts in the middle of the night when it's quiet and nobody else is around. He'll dangle a thought out in front of you and just hope you bite. But if you meditate on the Word day and night, you'll be able to stand strong and give no place to the enemy.

Third John 2 says, "...I pray for good fortune [or you could say good success] in everything you do, and for your good health—that your everyday affairs prosper, as well as your soul!" (The Message). Think about that. God is involved and cares about your everyday affairs.

But I'm just a speck on the earth, you might think. No, if you're born again, you are a child of God, and He loves and cares about every facet of your life. Wow! The God of the universe, the Creator of the world, cares about the things you care about.

God also is telling you that there's a direct correlation between success and spiritual growth. As you get full of God's Word and built-up praying in the Holy Ghost, you become more sensitive to God's voice. Everything about your life begins to prosper and fall in place. Yet, keep in mind, that there are no shortcuts to success. The world offers get-rich-quick schemes, but they won't take you where you want to go. There are also no short cuts in your walk with God, but if you do your part, God is always faithful to do His.

True success means different things to different people, but bottom line, true success means living the God-kind of life. When it comes down to it, if you don't live *The God Life*, you don't know real life at all. Don't settle for anything less.

ACTION ▷ ···

Find scriptures that cover your situation. Meditate on them. Eat them. Declare them. And watch things begin to change in your life because God is for sure watching over His Word to perform it in your life.

_____

_____

_____

_____

_____

(89) | HANDS IN THE AIR

We were created to praise God. In fact, God said, "This people have I formed for myself; they shall shew forth my praise," (Isaiah 43:21 KJV). That's a pretty heavy responsibility because it means we show forth His praise anywhere and everywhere we go. It means we should live a life of praise, which is not only praising God on an occasional Sunday morning. It's praising God day in and day out through good times and bad. It's praise flowing out of us like a river.

"Yeah, but, I'm not really given to praise. A lot of praise and worship makes me uncomfortable. I don't get very emotional." Yet, I don't find any place in my Bible where it says, "They shall show forth My praise if they're given to it, if they're comfortable, if it doesn't make too much noise." No, when it comes right down to it, the Bible doesn't invite you to praise or suggest you praise. The Bible just tells you to do it.

You'll never be really happy until you do because it's why you were created.

As Mark and I have traveled the nations for more than 35 years, we've heard many languages spoken, but there is only one universal word spoken: *Hallelujah!* I've often greeted Christians around the world saying *Hallelujah!* They understood me perfectly, and it was a starting place for good communication. Open your mouth and say it with me now, *Hallelujah. Hallelujah. Hallelujah!* It does the soul good to say it.

Now let's go a step further. While on vacation awhile back, I saw a commercial advertising a children's movie with little cartoon characters who had their hands in the air saying, "Wave your hands in the air like you just don't care." I thought, *Oh, yeah! I can do that!* So for the rest of our vacation, I walked around singing that little song and waving my hands in the air like I just didn't care.

It did me a world of good, and it will do the same for you. There are plenty of times you need to wave your hands in the air like you just don't even care because the Bible says we're not supposed to carry our cares. Cares can get really, really heavy. So what does the Bible say to do with our cares? "Casting the whole of your care [all your anxieties, all your worries, all your concerns, once and for all] on Him, for He cares for you affectionately *and* cares about you watchfully." (1 Peter 5:7 AMP).

You don't need to carry your cares. God will. If there's caring that needs to be done, He will do it. All you have to do is wave your hands in the air like you just don't even care.

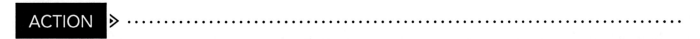

ACTION

Ok, hands in the air! Start waving! Start thanking God that as you cast your care on Him, He will take care of things. Let go of whatever has been dogging your trail. Let go of sickness. Let go of depression. Let go of fear. Every time a care starts to come back on you, just throw your hands in the air and wave them like you just don't even care.

Repeat as often as necessary.

(90) | EXTRAORDINARY NOT ORDINARY

In these last days before the Rapture of the Church, a lot of work needs to be done in order for God to reap His last great harvest, and God needs a lot of laborers to do the work. The good news is that God doesn't require a resume. He also doesn't choose people according to what they have been but according to what they can be. In fact, it doesn't take someone with great qualifications to do something great for God. First Corinthians 1:27 says, "…God hath chosen the foolish things of the world to confound the wise; and God hath chosen the weak things of the world to confound the things which are mighty" (KJV).

God is not looking for great ability. He's looking for availability. He has all the rest.

God needs *you*.

God is really looking for people like you who are hungry for more of Him because hungry people follow where He leads. Actually, what matters most is where you're willing to go in God. Once God finds a willing heart, the action begins. God takes ordinary people like you and me and makes them extraordinary.

God has always worked this way. He told Moses to stretch out his hand and part the waters. God empowered David to destroy a lion as well as a bear with his bare hands. Samson slew another 1000 men with the jawbone of a donkey, which beats any action hero you'll ever see in a comic book or movie.

God took the ordinary shepherd boy David and led him to defeat a giant. In the beginning, David didn't look like he had the makings of a leader. David was the youngest of seven, and when the prophet came to anoint a king, David's own father didn't even think to mention him. But God has a history of using unlikely people to do amazing things. Consider Esther. She was an ordinary Jewish girl, chosen to be queen. She was positioned by God for a purpose, and she saved her entire nation.

In the New Testament, we find a man named Saul who was a very unlikely candidate to write half of the New Testament. Saul, who became the apostle Paul, actually had a lot of strikes against him in the beginning, including a reputation for persecuting and killing Christians. But after an encounter with Jesus on the road to Damascus, everything changed.

Then there's you. God has big plans for you, too. Isaiah 14:24 says, "Surely, as I have thought, so it shall come to pass, And as I have purposed, so it shall stand." God has plans and purposes already planted in your heart, and they will come to pass. Find them. Follow them. Hold tight to Him and let Him lead the way.

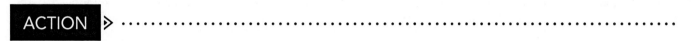

Ask God what His plans are for you, and then get ready! How? Get full of the Word and full of the Spirit. Be willing. Be obedient. And go live *The God Life*.

LIVING BEYOND THE ORDINARY

The best and most important decision you can make in this life is to receive Jesus Christ as your Lord and Savior. It's the way to eternal life with God in heaven ever after, and it's the gateway to living life beyond the ordinary here and now. There's no better way to live.

You can take this life-changing step today by praying this simple prayer aloud.

Dear heavenly Father:

Your Word says, "Whosoever shall call on the name of the Lord shall be saved" (Acts 2:21 KJV). I call on You right now.

The Bible also says if I confess with my mouth that Jesus is Lord and believe in my heart that You have raised Him from the dead, I shall be saved (Romans 10:9-10). I make that choice now.

Jesus, I believe in You. I believe in my heart and confess with my mouth that You were raised from the dead. I ask You to be my Lord and Savior. Thank You for forgiving me of all my sins. I believe I'm now a new creation in You. Old things have passed away; all things have become new in Jesus' name (2 Corinthians 5:17). Amen.

Share Your Good News

If you prayed this prayer today, please contact our office. We want to hear from you!

World Outreach Church
P.O. Box 470308
Tulsa, OK 74147-0308
918-461-9628
Prayer@woctulsa.org

WORLD OUTREACH CHURCH

8863 E. 91st St.
Tulsa, Oklahoma

Service times — www.woctulsa.org or 918.461.9628

Live streaming and archived services — www.woctulsa.org.

Teaching materials by Pastors Mark and Janet Brazee and music by Pastor Janet —
www.woctulsa.org.

We're a place *you* can call home!

CPSIA information can be obtained
at www.ICGtesting.com
Printed in the USA
FFOW05n1128261015

9 780989 142960